1-2-3® for DOS
Release 3.1+
Quick Reference

Brian Underdahl

que

1-2-3® for DOS 3.1+ Quick Reference.

Copyright ©1992 by Que Corporation.

All rights reserved. Printed in the United States of America. No part of this book may be used or reproduced in any form or by any means, or stored in a database or retrieval system, without prior written permission of the publisher except in the case of brief quotations embodied in critical articles and reviews. Making copies of any part of this book for any purpose other than your own personal use is a violation of United States copyright laws. For information, address Que Corporation, 11711 North College Avenue, Suite 140, Carmel, IN 46032.

Library of Congress Catalog Number: 91-62613

ISBN: 0-88022-845-8

This book is sold *as is*, without warranty of any kind, either express or implied, respecting the contents of this book, including but not limited to implied warranties for the book's quality, performance, merchantability, or fitness for any particular purpose. Neither Que Corporation nor its dealers or distributors shall be liable to the purchaser or any other person or entity with respect to any liability, loss, or damage caused or alleged to be caused directly or indirectly by this book.

94 93 92 91   4 3 2

Interpretation of the printing code: the rightmost double-digit number is the year of the book's printing; the rightmost single-digit number is the number of the book's printing. For example, a printing code of 92-4 shows that the fourth printing of the book occurred in 1992.

This book is based on Lotus 1-2-3 Releases 3, 3.1, and 3.1+.

Que Quick Reference Series

The *Que Quick Reference Series* is a portable resource of essential microcomputer knowledge. Drawing on the experience of many of Que's best-selling authors, this series helps you easily access important program information. The *Que Quick Reference Series* includes these titles:

1-2-3 for DOS Release 2.3 Quick Reference
1-2-3 for DOS Release 3.1+ Quick Reference
1-2-3 for Windows Quick Reference
1-2-3 Release 2.2 Quick Reference
Allways Quick Reference
AutoCAD Quick Reference, 2nd Edition
Batch Files and Macros Quick Reference
CheckFree Quick Reference
CorelDRAW! Quick Reference
dBASE IV Quick Reference
Excel for Windows Quick Reference
Fastback Quick Reference
Hard Disk Quick Reference
Harvard Graphics Quick Reference
LapLink Quick Reference
Microsoft Word 5 Quick Reference
Microsoft Word Quick Reference
Microsoft Works Quick Reference
MS-DOS 5 Quick Reference
MS-DOS Quick Reference
Norton Utilities Quick Reference
Paradox Quick Reference
PC Tools 7 Quick Reference
Q&A 4 Quick Reference
Quark XPress Quick Reference
Quattro Pro Quick Reference
Quicken Quick Reference
System 7 Quick Reference
UNIX Programmer's Quick Reference
UNIX Shell Commands Quick Reference
Windows 3 Quick Reference
WordPerfect 5.1 Quick Reference
WordPerfect for Windows Quick Reference
WordPerfect Quick Reference

Publisher
Lloyd J. Short

Series Director
Karen A. Bluestein

Production Editor
Pamela D. Wampler

Editorial Assistants
Hilary Adams
Patricia J. Brooks

Technical Editor
Joyce J. Nielsen

Production Team
Denny Hager
Phil Kitchel
Bob LaRoche
Juli Pavey
Susan VandeWalle

Trademark Acknowledgments

1-2-3 and Symphony are registered trademarks of Lotus Development Corporation.

dBASE and dBASE III are registered trademarks of Ashton-Tate Corporation.

Epson is a registered trademark of Epson America, Inc.

MS-DOS is a registered trademark of Microsoft Corporation.

Table of Contents

INTRODUCTION .... **x**

WORKSHEET BASICS **1**
   1-2-3 Keys 1
   Using a Mouse 6

ENTERING AND EDITING DATA **9**
   Entering Labels 9
   Entering Numbers 10
   Entering Formulas 10
   Editing Cell Contents 12

1-2-3 COMMAND REFERENCE **13**
   /Copy 13
   /Data Distribution 14
   /Data External Create 15
   /Data External Delete/Reset 15
   /Data External List 16
   /Data External Other 16
   /Data External Use 18
   /Data Fill 18
   /Data Matrix 19
   /Data Parse 19
   /Data Query Criteria 20
   /Data Query Delete 21
   /Data Query Extract/Unique 21
   /Data Query Find 22
   /Data Query Input 23
   /Data Query Modify 23
   /Data Query Output 24
   /Data Regression 25
   /Data Sort 25
   /Data Table 1/2/3 26

/Data Table Labeled	27
/File Admin Link-Refresh	28
/File Admin Reservation	29
/File Admin Seal	29
/File Admin Table	30
/File Combine	30
/File Dir	31
/File Erase	31
/File Import	31
/File List	32
/File New	33
/File Open	33
/File Retrieve	33
/File Save	34
/File Xtract	35
/Graph X/A/B/C/D/E/F	36
/Graph Group	37
/Graph Name	37
/Graph Options Advanced Colors	38
/Graph Options Advanced Hatches	39
/Graph Options Advanced Text	39
/Graph Options Color/B&W	40
/Graph Options Data-Labels	41
/Graph Options Format	41
/Graph Options Grid	42
/Graph Options Legend	42
/Graph Options Scale	43
/Graph Options Titles	43
/Graph Reset	44
/Graph Save	44
/Graph Type	44
/Graph View	46
/Move	46
/Print	47
/Print Printer/File/Encoded	47

/Print Printer Align	48
/Print Printer Clear	49
/Print Printer Hold	49
/Print Printer Image	50
/Print Printer Line	50
/Print Printer Options Advanced	51
/Print Printer Options Borders	54
/Print Printer Options Footer/Header	54
/Print Printer Options Margins	55
/Print Printer Options Name	55
/Print Printer Options Other	57
/Print Printer Options Pg-Length	57
/Print Printer Options Setup	57
/Print Printer Page	58
/Print Printer Range	58
/Print Printer Sample	59
/Quit	59
/Range Erase	60
/Range Format	60
/Range Input	63
/Range Justify	63
/Range Label	64
/Range Name	64
/Range Prot/Unprot	66
/Range Search	67
/Range Trans	67
/Range Value	68
/System	69
/Worksheet Column	70
/Worksheet Delete	70
/Worksheet Erase	71
/Worksheet Global Col-Width	71
/Worksheet Global Default	71
/Worksheet Global Format	74
/Worksheet Global Group	74

/Worksheet Global Label 75
/Worksheet Global Prot 75
/Worksheet Global Recalc 76
/Worksheet Global Zero 77
/Worksheet Hide 78
/Worksheet Insert 78
/Worksheet Page 79
/Worksheet Status 79
/Worksheet Titles 79
/Worksheet Window 80

WYSIWYG COMMAND REFERENCE 81

:Display Colors 82
:Display Default 83
:Display Font-Directory 84
:Display Mode 85
:Display Options 85
:Display Rows 87
:Display Zoom 88
:Format Bold 89
:Format Color 89
:Format Font 90
:Format Italics 91
:Format Lines 92
:Format Reset 93
:Format Shade 94
:Format Underline 94
:Graph Add 95
:Graph Compute 97
:Graph Edit 97
:Graph Goto 99
:Graph Move 99
:Graph Remove 100
:Graph Settings 101
:Graph View 103
:Graph Zoom 103

:Named-Style 104
:Print Configuration 105
:Print File 106
:Print Go 107
:Print Info 108
:Print Layout 108
:Print Preview 111
:Print Range 111
:Print Settings 112
:Quit 113
:Special Copy 114
:Special Export 114
:Special Import 115
:Special Move 116
:Text Align 117
:Text Clear 117
:Text Edit 118
:Text Reformat 119
:Text Set 119
:Worksheet Column 120
:Worksheet Page 121
:Worksheet Row 122

1-2-3 RELEASE 3.1+ ENHANCEMENT ADD-INS 123

The Auditor Add-In 123
The Backsolver Add-In 126
The Solver Add-In 127
The Viewer Add-In 131

1-2-3 FUNCTIONS 133

MACRO KEY NAMES 137

ADVANCED MACRO COMMANDS 139

INDEX 143

Introduction

1-2-3 for DOS Release 3.1+ Quick Reference is not a rehash of traditional documentation. Instead, this quick reference is a compilation of the most frequently used information from Que's best-selling 1-2-3 books.

1-2-3 for DOS Release 3.1+ Quick Reference presents essential information on 1-2-3 commands, @functions, and macros. You will learn the proper use of primary 1-2-3 functions and the new Wysiwyg commands that will help you enhance your spreadsheets. *1-2-3 for DOS Release 3.1+ Quick Reference* contains fundamental information in a compact, easy-to-use format.

Although *1-2-3 for DOS Release 3.1+ Quick Reference* contains essential 1-2-3 information, this information is not intended as a replacement for the comprehensive information presented in a full-size guide. You should supplement this quick reference with one of Que's complete 1-2-3 texts, such as *Using 1-2-3 for DOS Release 3.1+*, Special Edition.

Now you can put essential information at your fingertips with *1-2-3 for DOS Release 3.1+ Quick Reference*—and the entire *Que Quick Reference Series*!

WORKSHEET BASICS

Lotus 1-2-3 is used to perform repetitive math calculations, analyze data, manage files, and draw graphs.

1-2-3 commands are used for functions such as copying or moving portions of the worksheet, formatting cells to display currency, and using the database. You access 1-2-3 commands through a variety of menus.

Some menus and commands ask you to enter text or cell-address information. Other prompts request just text. After you supply an answer to a prompt, press Enter.

The *command line*, the second line on the screen, shows the current menu selections. To choose a menu item, press ← or → until your choice is highlighted, then press Enter. A quicker method is to type the first character of the menu item.

If you use the arrow keys to select a menu item, note that the cell pointer "wraps around" the end of the menu line in either direction.

As you use 1-2-3, watch the *prompt line*, which is the third line. If you make an incorrect selection from a menu, press Esc to back up to the preceding menu.

1-2-3 Keys

Pointer Keys

Move the cell pointer in the worksheet, across worksheets in a file, and across active files. Many of the same keys move the cursor in EDIT mode. Use the Num Lock key to toggle between pointer movement and 10-key entry.

For a key combination such as Shift-Tab, press and hold the first key, and then quickly press the second key. A plus sign between key names means you should press the two keys in turn and not simultaneously.

Pointer Keys with One Worksheet

Key(s)	Function
←	Moves the cell pointer left one cell.
→	Moves the cell pointer right one cell.
↑	Moves the cell pointer up one cell.
↓	Moves the cell pointer down one cell.
Ctrl-← or **Shift-Tab**	Moves the cell pointer one screen to the left.
Ctrl-→ or **Tab**	Moves the cell pointer one screen to the right.
End+←	Moves the cell pointer to the left.*
End+→	Moves the cell pointer to the right.*
End+↑	Moves the cell pointer up.*
End+↓	Moves the cell pointer down.*
End+Home	Moves the cell pointer to the lowest right corner of the active area.
Home	Moves the pointer to the upper left corner of the worksheet (cell A1 in normal operation) or to the upper left unfixed cell when titles are fixed with **/W**orksheet **T**itles.
Num Lock	Toggles the numeric keypad from pointer movement to numeric entry.
PgUp	Moves the cell pointer up one screen.
PgDn	Moves the cell pointer down one screen.

Worksheet Basics

F5 (GoTo) — Prompts for a cell address or range name, and then moves the cell pointer directly to that cell (which can be in another worksheet or file).

F6 (Window) — If the window is split, moves the cell pointer to the next window (which can be in another worksheet or file).

Scroll Lock — Toggles on and off the scroll function; when on, moves the entire window when you press one of the four arrow keys.

*Moves the cell pointer in the direction of the arrow to the next intersection between a blank cell and a cell that contains data.

Additional Pointer Keys with Multiple Worksheets

Key(s)	Function
Ctrl-PgUp	Moves the cell pointer to the next worksheet.
Ctrl-PgDn	Moves the cell pointer to the preceding worksheet.
Ctrl-Home	Moves the cell pointer to the home position in the first worksheet in the file (usually A:A1).
End+Ctrl-Home	Moves the cell pointer to the end of the active area for the file in the last worksheet.
End+Ctrl-PgUp or **End+Ctrl-PgDn**	Moves the cell pointer through the worksheets to the next intersection between a blank cell and a cell that contains data.
Ctrl-End+Ctrl-PgUp	Moves the cell pointer to the next file.

Key(s)	Function
Ctrl-End+ Ctrl-PgDn	Moves the cell pointer to the preceding file.
Ctrl-End+ Home	Moves the cell pointer to the first file in memory.
Ctrl-End+ End	Moves the cell pointer to the last file in memory.

Function Keys

Function keys save you time as you perform special tasks. Depending on the hardware, function keys are labeled F1 through F10. Some keyboards have twelve function keys. 1-2-3 uses only the first ten.

Following is a list of function keys and function-key combinations.

F1 (Help) accesses the on-line help facility.

F2 (Edit) places 1-2-3 in EDIT mode so that you can change the current cell.

F3 (Name) displays a list of names any time a command or formula can accept a range name or a file name. After you type @ in a formula, displays a list of functions. After you type a left brace ({) in a label, displays a list of macro key names and advanced macro commands.

F4 (Abs) changes a cell or range address from relative to absolute to mixed and back to relative.

F5 (GoTo) moves the cell pointer to a specified cell address or range name.

F6 (Window) moves the cell pointer to another window or worksheet when the screen is split.

F7 (Query) in READY mode, repeats the last **/D**ata **Q**uery command. During a **/D**ata **Q**uery **F**ind, switches between FIND and READY modes.

F8 (Table) repeats the last **/D**ata **T**able command.

F9 (Calc) in READY mode, recalculates all worksheets in memory. If entering or editing a formula, converts the formula to its current value.

Worksheet Basics

F10 (Graph) displays the current graph. If no current graph exists, displays the data around the cell pointer.

Alt-F1 (Compose) creates international characters that cannot be typed directly with the keyboard.

Alt-F2 (Record) enables you to save up to 512 keystrokes in a cell or to repeat a series of commands. Also toggles on and off macro STEP mode.

Alt-F3 (Run) runs a macro.

Alt-F4 (Undo) reverses the last action.

Alt-F6 (Zoom) enlarges a split window to full size.

Alt-F7 (App1) starts a 1-2-3 add-in assigned to this key.

Alt-F8 (App2) starts a 1-2-3 add-in assigned to this key.

Alt-F9 (App3) starts a 1-2-3 add-in assigned to this key.

Alt-F10 (Addin) accesses 1-2-3 add-ins.

Other Special 1-2-3 Keys

Backspace

During cell definition or editing, erases the preceding character. Cancels old ranges shown in some prompts. Displays the preceding Help Screen if you are using Help.

/ (slash) **or** < (less-than sign)

Starts a command from READY mode. Used as the division when data is entered or a formula is edited in a cell.

. (period)

When used in a range address, separates the address of the cell at the beginning of the range from the address of the cell at the end of the range. In POINT mode, moves the anchor cell to another corner of the range.

Break

Cancels a macro or cancels menu choices and returns to READY mode.

Esc

When accessing the command menus, cancels the current menu and returns to the preceding menu. Returns to READY mode if at the Main menu. Clears the edit line when entering or editing data in a cell. Cancels a range during some prompts that display the old range. Returns from the on-line help facility.

Using a Mouse

You can use a mouse with 1-2-3 Releases 3.1 and 3.1+ if the mouse driver is installed and Wysiwyg is loaded into memory. To install your mouse driver, see the documentation that came with your mouse. To install Wysiwyg, use the procedure outlined in the Wysiwyg section of this book.

Reminder

When you move the mouse pointer to the Control panel, the 1-2-3 Main menu or the Wysiwyg Main menu, whichever you last used, appears. Click the right mouse button to toggle between these menus.

To select icons with the mouse

When you use a mouse, 1-2-3 displays icons in the icon panel located to the right of the worksheet area. You can select icons with the mouse. The icon panel contains the following icons.

◀   Moves the cell pointer left in the current worksheet.

▶   Moves the cell pointer right in the current worksheet.

▲   Moves the cell pointer up in the current worksheet.

▼   Moves the cell pointer down in the current worksheet.

↑   Moves the cell pointer to the next worksheet or file in memory.

| ↓ | Moves the cell pointer to the previous worksheet or file in memory. |
| ? | Displays help. |

To move the cell pointer with a mouse

You can move the cell pointer with a mouse as well as with the pointer keys when Wysiwyg is in memory.

To move the cell pointer to a cell with the mouse, click that cell with the left mouse button.

To move the cell pointer around the worksheet, position the mouse pointer on top of the cell pointer, press and hold the left mouse button, and move, or drag, the cell pointer to another location in the worksheet. Release the button.

Move the cell pointer by clicking the triangle and arrow icons that appear in the icon panel. Click the triangles with the left mouse button to move the cell pointer in the direction that a triangle points within a worksheet. Click the arrow icons with the left button to move forward and backward through multiple worksheets. If you click an icon once, the cell pointer moves to the next cell or worksheet. Press and hold the left button to scroll continuously. Release the button to stop scrolling.

To select menu commands

You can use the mouse to select commands from either the 1-2-3 Main menu or the Wysiwyg Main menu.

1. Move the mouse pointer to the Control panel.

2. To switch to the opposite menu (if necessary), click the right mouse button.

3. Click the command with the left mouse button.

4. To return 1-2-3 to READY mode, move the mouse pointer to the worksheet.

To specify a single-sheet range with a mouse

1. Move the mouse pointer to a corner cell of the range you want to specify.

2. Press and hold the left mouse button to anchor the cell pointer.

3. Drag the mouse pointer to the corner diagonally opposite and release the button.

4. Click the left mouse button to specify the range.

5. To cancel the highlighted range, click the right mouse button.

To specify a multiple-sheet range with a mouse

1. Highlight a single-sheet range, following Steps 1 through 3 above.

2. Click the up-arrow icon in the icon panel to move backward through worksheets, or the down-arrow icon to move forward through worksheets.

3. Click the icon once with the left mouse button for each worksheet you want to add to the range.

4. Click the left mouse button to specify the range.

5. To cancel the highlighted range, click the right mouse button.

To highlight a range before selecting a command

You can highlight a range before you select a Wysiwyg command (but not a 1-2-3 Main menu command). You can use this technique with the Wysiwyg **:F**ormat and **:T**ext commands.

1. Position the cell pointer in one corner of the range you want to specify.

2. To anchor the cell pointer, press **F4**.

3. Click and hold the left mouse button and drag the mouse to the opposite corner of the range.

4. Release the button.

5. Type **:**.

6. Select a Wysiwyg command.

7. Select any other commands you want.

8. Press **Esc**, move the cell pointer, or click the left mouse button when you no longer want to work with the range.

ENTERING AND EDITING DATA

The following section tells you how to enter labels (text), numbers, and formulas into a cell. It also explains how to modify existing cell contents.

After you type the first character of an entry, 1-2-3 determines the type of entry. If the entry is text, the mode indicator changes to LABEL. If the entry is the beginning of a number or formula, VALUE mode is activated.

Entering Labels

To enter a label

Type the label into the cell. If the label starts with one of the following numeric characters

0 1 2 3 4 5 6 7 8 9 . + − $ (@ #

you must precede the label with a label prefix. The label prefix tells 1-2-3 that the entry is a label and indicates how the text is aligned in the cell. If you do not start the entry with a label prefix and the entry starts with one of the numeric characters, 1-2-3 considers the entry a value.

Notes

Following are label prefixes you can use to control alignment:

Label Prefix	Function
' (apostrophe)	Aligns label to the left (default setting).
" (quotation mark)	Aligns label to the right.
^ (caret)	Centers label in the cell.
\ (backslash)	Repeats character to fill a cell.*

Label Prefix	Function
| (vertical bar)	Aligns label to the left, and does not print it.*

*This prefix cannot be selected with **/WGL** or **/RL**.

You can change the default label prefix with **/W**orksheet **G**lobal **L**abel-Prefix. You may use this to change only new labels. To change the alignment of existing labels, you can use **/R**ange **L**abel.

Entering Numbers

To enter a number

Start typing with one of the following characters:

0 1 2 3 4 5 6 7 8 9 . + – $

To attach an explanatory note to a number

Type a semicolon (;) after the number, followed by the note.

Entering Formulas

To enter a formula

Start the entry with one of the following numbers or symbols:

0 1 2 3 4 5 6 7 8 9 . + – $ (@ #

If you start the entry with any other character, 1-2-3 assumes the entry is a label.

Use operators to specify the calculations that 1-2-3 is to perform. Use parentheses to change the order of precedence (the order in which the operators are evaluated).

To attach an explanatory note to the formula, type a semicolon (;) at the end, followed by the note.

Entering and Editing Data

Notes

Numeric formulas operate on numbers; string formulas operate on text; and logical formulas compare two entries. The result of a logical test is TRUE or FALSE. TRUE has a value of 1, and FALSE has a value of 0.

Following is a list of items included in formulas:

Item	*Description*
@functions	Predefined formulas.
Addresses	Cell addresses or range names.
Operators	Symbols, such as + and –, for numeric, string, or logical operations.
Numbers	Used for math calculations.
Strings	Text used in string formulas.

Following is a list of numeric operators:

Operator	*Meaning*	*Precedence*
^	Exponentiation (to the power of)	1
+, –	Positive, Negative	2
*, /	Multiplication, Division	3
+, –	Addition, Subtraction	4
=, <>	Equal, Not equal	5
<, >	Less than, Greater than	5
<=	Less than or equal to	5
>=	Greater than or equal to	5

Operator	Meaning	Precedence
#NOT#	Logical NOT; reverses a true/false result	6
#AND#	Logical AND	7
#OR#	Logical OR	7

Notes

The order of precedence is indicated from the top of the list downward.

Following is a list of string operators:

Operator	Function
+	Repeats the string or cell addresses. This operator must be used only once, at the beginning of the formula.
&	Concatenates a string to the preceding string (adds it to the end).

To place a string inside a formula, enclose it in double quotes.

Editing Cell Contents

Use the Backspace key to correct a typing error while you are entering data. Press **F2** (Edit) to modify long entries or existing cell contents.

To write over existing cell contents

You may ignore the contents of a cell and type a new entry; the new entry replaces the old entry when you press **Enter**. To cancel the new entry and keep the old entry, press **Esc** before you press **Enter**.

To edit cell contents

1. Press **F2** (Edit). The cell contents appear on the second line of the screen. The flashing cursor indicates where your typing will be placed. If the

entry is too long to be displayed on one line, the edit area expands to display the entire entry.

2. Use the edit keys to make any changes.

3. When you finish editing, press **Enter** (the cursor can be anywhere in the edit line at this time).

1-2-3 COMMAND REFERENCE

The 1-2-3 Command Reference includes all the 1-2-3 commands available when you press slash (/).

Each command is followed by an explanation of its purpose and reminders of any preparation required before activating the command. The procedures are indicated in a step-by-step manner. Keystrokes within the text you type are in **blue**. A "notes" section contains additional comments, information, hints, or suggestions for using the command.

Note: When you type the designated letter to select a command, the letter does not have to be capitalized.

/Copy

Purpose

Copies formulas, values, labels, formats, and cell-protection attributes to new locations.

Reminder

Make sure that you have enough space on your worksheets to receive the cell or range of cells being copied. For three-dimensional copies, you must have enough room in the TO: range to hold the entire duplicate. Copies replace the preceding cell contents.

To copy data

1. Type **/C**.

2. The FROM: prompt requests the range of the cells to be copied. Highlight a range, or type the range name or the range address. Press **Enter**.

3. At the TO: prompt, specify the upper left corner of the top worksheet where you want the duplicate to appear by moving the cell pointer to that position. Press the period key (.) to anchor the first corner. If you want multiple adjacent duplicates or duplicates across worksheets and files, highlight additional cells that define the upper left corners of the additional duplicates and press **Enter**.

/Data Distribution

Purpose

Creates a frequency distribution showing how often specific data occur in a database.

Reminders

/DD works only on numeric values.

Data must be arranged in a column, row, or rectangular range. This is called the *value range*.

Move the cell pointer to a worksheet portion that has two adjacent blank columns. In the left column, enter the highest value for each entry in the bin range. Enter these bin values in ascending order.

To create a frequency distribution

1. Type **/DD**.

2. Enter the value range, which contains the data being analyzed.

3. Enter the bin range.

The frequency distribution appears in the column to the right of the bin range. Note that the frequency column extends one row beyond the bin range.

See also /Data Fill.

/Data External Create

Purpose

Creates the structure for a new external database table. The new database contains only field names.

To create an external database table
1. Type **/DE**.

2. Select **N**ame to establish a connection between 1-2-3 and the external database, and assign a name to the table. Specify the database driver you want to use. Then enter a range name of up to 15 characters and press **Enter**. You may enter a table creation string. If you do not have a table creation string, press **Enter**.

3. Select **D**efinition **U**se-Definition and specify the range containing the six-column table definition. Include all rows for the fields you want in the table.

4. Select **G**o.

/Data External Delete/Reset

Purpose

/DED deletes a table from an external database, and /DER breaks the link to an external database table.

Reminder

/DED can be used even if a link has not been established to an external table via the **E**xternal **U**se command.

To delete an external database table
1. Type **/DED**.

2. Specify the name of the external database.

3. Specify the name of the table in the external database.

4. Select **Y**es to delete the table or **N**o to keep the table.

To break the link to an external database table

Type **/DER**, and then specify the range name of the link you want to break.

/Data External List

Purpose

Lists the tables and fields in an external database. Use these lists with the **/D**ata **Q**uery commands to create criteria and output ranges to extract information from the external database.

Reminder

A range name must be assigned to the external database before you can use /DEL. Use **/D**ata **E**xternal **U**se to create that range.

To list tables and fields in an external database

1. Type **/DEL**.

2. Select **F**ields to extract the field names used in the external table.

3. Specify the name of the external table and location where you want the field names to be copied.

4. Select **Q**uit to return to the worksheet.

5. Use **/R**ange **T**rans to convert the column of field names to a row of field headings.

/Data External Other

Purpose

Sends commands directly to an external database to control the database, to update worksheet Query or Table functions, or to translate data using foreign character sets.

1-2-3 Command Reference

Reminder

Before using /DEO, use **/D**ata **E**xternal **U**se to establish a link to an external database. Some database drivers may not enable the use of **O**ther.

To update a worksheet linked to an external database

1. Type **/DEO**.

2. Select **R**efresh.

3. Choose one of the following:

Menu Item	Function
Automatic	Updates the worksheet's data from the external database and recalculates the worksheet using the time interval you specify with the **R**efresh **I**nterval command.
Interval	Sets the frequency with which updates occur. Enter the number of seconds from **0** to **36,000** (one hour). The default is 1 second.
Manual	Prevents **/D**ata **Q**uery commands, **/D**ata **T**able commands, and worksheet recalculations from being updated automatically.

To send commands to an external database

1. Type **/DEO**.

2. Select **C**ommand.

3. Specify the database driver.

4. Specify the name of the external database.

5. Enter a command or the cell address containing a command as a label. These commands appear in your database driver documentation or in the database documentation.

To translate an external database using foreign character sets

1. Type **/DEO**.

2. Select Translation.
3. Specify the name of the database driver.
4. Specify the name of the database table to translate.
5. Specify the name of a character.

/Data External Use

Purpose

Links 1-2-3 database capabilities to an external database table created by another program.

Reminder

You must make a link to an external table and assign a range name before 1-2-3 can use the table's information.

To use an external database

1. Type /DEU.

2. Select the name of the database driver to use. Use SAMPLE to use the dBASE III driver that comes with 1-2-3.

3. Specify the path containing the external database you want to use. Specify the database you want to use. Use EMPFILE to use the sample dBASE file that comes with 1-2-3.

4. Specify a range name for the database you select. The range name can contain up to 15 characters.

/Data Fill

Purpose

Fills a specified range with a series of equally incremented numbers, dates, times, or percentages.

Use /DF to create date rows or columns, numeric rows or columns, headings for depreciation tables, sensitivity analyses, data tables, or databases.

1-2-3 Command Reference

Reminder

Numbers generated by /DF overwrite previous entries.

To fill a range

1. Type /DF.

2. Specify the range to be filled.

3. Enter the start number, date, or time in the filled range and press Enter. You can reference a cell or range that results in a value. The default value is 0.

4. When a Step value is requested, type the positive or negative number by which you want the value to be incremented. Date or time Step values can use special units. The default value is 1.

5. Enter a Stop value.

/Data Matrix

Purpose

Inverts columns and rows in square matrices. Multiplies column-and-row matrices of cells.

To invert a matrix

1. Type /DM.

2. Choose Invert to invert a nonsingular square matrix of up to 90 rows and columns.

3. Specify the range you want to invert. Press Enter.

4. Specify an output range to hold the inverted solution matrix. Press Enter.

/Data Parse

Purpose

Separates the long labels resulting from /File Import into distinct text and numeric cell entries. The separated text and numbers are placed in individual cells in a row of an output range.

To parse data

1. Move the cell pointer to the first cell in the row where you want to begin parsing.

2. Type **/DP**.

3. Select **F**ormat-Line.

4. Select **C**reate. A format line is inserted at the cell pointer, and the row of data moves down. This format line shows 1-2-3's "best guess" at how the data in the cell pointer should be separated.

5. You may need to change the format line to include or exclude data by selecting **E**dit from the **F**ormat-Line menu. Edit the format line and press **Enter**.

6. If the imported data is in different formats—an uneven number of items or a mixture of field names and numbers, for example—you must create additional format lines. Enter these lines at the row where the data format changed.

7. Select **I**nput-Column.

8. Specify the column containing the format line and the data you want to format.

9. Select **O**utput-Range.

10. Move the cell pointer to the upper left corner of the range to receive the parsed data and press **Enter**.

11. Select **G**o.

/Data Query Criteria

Purpose

Specifies the worksheet range containing the criteria that defines which records you want to find.

======= 1-2-3 Command Reference =======

Reminder

Indicate a criteria range before you use the **F**ind, **E**xtract, **U**nique, **D**el, or **M**odify options of the **/DQ** command.

To specify a criteria range

Type **/DQC**. Then specify or highlight the range that will contain field names and criteria. The range must contain at least two rows: the first row includes field names from the top row of the database you want to search, and the second row includes the criteria you specify.

/Data Query Delete

Purpose

Removes from the input range any records that meet conditions in the criteria range.

"Cleans up" your database by removing records that are not current or that you extracted to another worksheet.

Reminders

You must define a 1-2-3 database complete with input and criteria ranges.

Use **/D**ata **Q**uery **F**ind to ensure that your criteria is accurate before deleting those records that meet the specified conditions.

To remove database records

Type **/DQD**.

/Data Query Extract/Unique

Purpose

Copies to the output range of the worksheet records that meet conditions set in the criteria. With /DQU, copies only nonduplicate records and sorts them.

Reminder

You must define a 1-2-3 database complete with input, output, and criteria ranges.

To copy records

Type **/DQE** to copy all records that meet the conditions set in the criteria.

Type **/DQU** to copy nonduplicate records that meet conditions set in the criteria and to sort the copied records.

/Data Query Find

Purpose

Finds records in the database that meet conditions you set in the criteria range.

Reminders

/DQF works only with a single input range.

You must define the input range, external table (if one is used), and criteria range before using /DQF.

To find database records

1. Type **/DQF**.

   The cell pointer highlights the first record that meets the criteria. You will hear a beep if no record in the input range meets the criteria.

2. Press ↑ or ↓ to move to the next record that meets the criteria. Press **Home** or **End** to find the first or last record in the database that meets the criteria.

3. You can edit contents within a record. When the cell pointer highlights the cell you want to edit, press **F2** and edit the cell contents. Press **Enter**.

/Data Query Input

Purpose

Specifies a range of data records to be searched.

Reminders

You must indicate an input range before you use the **F**ind, **E**xtract, **U**nique, **D**el, or **M**odify options of the **/DQ** command.

The input range can be within a worksheet's data table or within an external table and must include the field names. You can specify more than one input range.

To specify a range of records to be searched

1. Type **/DQI**.

2. Specify the range of data records you want to search. Be sure to include in the range the field names at the top of the range and portions of the records that may be off the screen.

3. To specify more than one data table, use an argument separator—a comma (**,**), period (**.**), or semicolon (**;**)—to separate input ranges. After you specify all the databases, press **Enter**.

/Data Query Modify

Purpose

Inserts or replaces records in the input range with records from the output range.

Selects a group of records, edits them, and inserts them again into the database table.

Reminders

Before using the **E**xtract and **R**eplace options of /DQM, you must specify input, output, and criteria ranges.

The Replace command can replace a formula in the input range with a value from the output range. Be careful not to change formulas to values in your database.

To extract, insert, or replace records

1. Type /DQM.

2. Select Extract, Replace, Insert, or Cancel.

3. If you choose Extract, you can modify the records in the output range. At Step 1, choose Replace or Insert to update the input range when you are finished.

/Data Query Output

Purpose

Assigns a location to which found records can be copied by using the Extract, Unique, or Modify commands.

Reminders

You must indicate an output range before you use the Extract, Unique, or Modify options of the /DQ command. The Find and Delete options do not use an output range.

If the input range includes multiple database tables with the same field names, precede field names in the output range with the database name (DB2.AMOUNT and DB3.AMOUNT, for example).

To specify an output range

Type /DQO. Then specify the output field names. If you want a limited number of extracted records, the number of rows in the output range should be equal to the number of extracted rows you want.

/Data Regression

Purpose

Finds trends in data, using multiple linear regression techniques.

Reminder

The output area must be at least nine rows, and must be two columns wider than the number of sets of x values (no less than four columns wide).

To find trends in data

1. Type /DR.

2. Select X-Range, then specify the range, which may contain up to 75 independent variables. The values must be in adjacent columns.

3. Select Y-Range and specify the range containing a single column of dependent variables. This single column must have the same number of rows as the X-range.

4. Select Intercept and choose Compute or Zero.

5. Select Output-Range and enter the cell address of the upper left corner of the output range.

6. Select Go to calculate the regression.

/Data Sort

Purpose

Sorts the database in ascending or descending order.

Reminders

Sorting can be done on one or more fields (columns).

Do not include blank rows or the data labels at the top of the database when you highlight the data range. Blank rows will sort to the top or bottom of the database, and the data labels will sort into the body of the database.

To sort a database

1. Type /DS.

2. Highlight the data range to be sorted. You must include every field (column) in the database, but do not include the field labels at the top of the database (this will cause the labels to be sorted with the data). Press Enter.

3. Move the cell pointer to the column of the database that will be the Primary-Key and press Enter.

4. Specify Ascending or Descending order.

5. Select the Secondary-Key if you want to sort duplicate copies of the Primary-Key.

6. Specify Ascending or Descending order.

7. Select Extra-Key if you want to sort additional keys. Enter the number of the extra key (from 3 to 253). Enter a cell address in the column on which this key will sort.

8. Specify Ascending or Descending order.

9. Repeat Steps 7 and 8 to sort additional keys.

10. Select Go.

/Data Table 1/2/3

Purpose

Generates a table composed of one, two, or three varying input values and the result from single or multiple formulas. These commands are useful for generating "what if" models.

Reminder

Use /DT1 to show how changes in one variable affect the output from one or more formulas. Use /DT2 to show how changes in two variables affect the output from one formula. Use /DT3 to show how changes in three variables affect the output from one formula.

To create a data table

1. Type **/DT1, /DT2,** or **/DT3**.

2. For /DT1, enter the table range so that it includes the Input 1 values or text in the extreme left column and the formulas in the top row.

   For /DT2, enter the table range so that it includes the Input 1 values in the extreme left column and the Input 2 values in the top row.

   For /DT3, enter the table range so that it includes the Input 1 values in the extreme left column, the Input 2 values in the top row, and the Input 3 values at the top left corner. Press **Ctrl-PgDn** to extend the range to additional worksheets at lower levels. Then enter the address for the formula cell.

3. Enter the address for Input 1.

   For /DT2 and /DT3, enter the address for Input 2.

   For /DT3, enter the address for Input 3.

1-2-3 places the Input value(s) into the designated cell(s), recalculates each formula, and places the results in the data table.

/Data Table Labeled

Purpose

/DTL is a more flexible method than the /DT1, /DT2, or /DT3 method to create tables that test input changes on formulas. Although /DTL enables greater analysis, it is more complex to create.

Reminder

The formula labels at the top of the data table label range must match the labels above each formula. Use **/C**opy to create exact duplicates of the formula labels.

To create a labeled data table

1. Type /DTL.

2. Select Formulas and specify the range containing the formulas and the labels over the formulas. Enter the formula label range that defines the width of the table.

3. Select Down and specify the row variable range. Confirm this range by pressing Enter again. Specify the cell for Input 1.

4. Select Across and specify the column variable range. Confirm this range by pressing Enter again. Specify the cell for Input 2.

5. Select Sheets and specify the worksheet variable range. Use Ctrl-PgUp to specify that the range include other worksheets. Confirm this range by pressing Enter again. Specify the cell for Input 3.

6. Select Input-Cells if you want to review or change any of the variable ranges and the corresponding input cells.

7. Select Go to calculate and fill the table.

/File Admin Link-Refresh

Purpose

Recalculates formulas in the active files that depend on data in other active files or files on disk.

Ensures that your worksheet is using current data when the files are shared between users (on a network, for example).

Reminder

Use /FAL before printing or reviewing final results if the current file is linked to other files that may have changed.

To recalculate formulas that depend upon data in other files

Type /FAL.

/File Admin Reservation

Purpose

Controls the reservation status of a shared file on a network. A reservation is the ability to write to a file with the same file name.

To modify the reservation status of a shared file

Type **/FAR**. Then choose from **G**et, **R**elease, or **S**etting (Manual or Automatic). If you changed the file setting, save the file using **/F**ile **S**ave to save the new setting.

/File Admin Seal

Purpose

Protects a file's format or file reservation setting from changes.

Sealing a file also seals the settings that result from these commands: **/F**ile **A**dmin **R**eservation-Setting, **/G**raph **N**ame, **/P**rint **N**ame, **/R**ange [**F**ormat, **L**abel, **N**ame, **N**ame **N**ote, **P**rot, **U**nprot], and **/W**orksheet [**C**olumn, **H**ide, **G**lobal].

Reminder

To set up a file for data entry, while protecting formulas and macros, use **/R**ange **U**nprot to mark ranges to receive data, and choose **/W**orksheet **G**lobal **P**rot for worksheet protection. Seal the file to prevent unauthorized changes to the protected ranges.

To protect a file's format or reservation setting

1. Type **/FAS**.
2. Choose from **D**isable, **F**ile, or **R**eservation-Setting.
3. Type a password and press **Enter**.
4. If you are sealing the file or reservation setting, enter the password again and press **Enter**.

/File Admin Table

Purpose

Enters a table of files, which you select, in the worksheet.

To enter a table of files

1. Type **/FAT**.

2. Choose **A**ctive, **G**raph, **L**inked, **O**ther, **P**rint, or **W**orksheet.

3. If you choose **W**orksheet, **G**raph, **P**rint, or **O**ther, press **Enter** to enter a table for the current directory. If you want a table from another directory, type the directory name and press **Enter**.

4. Highlight the range where you want to place the table and press **Enter**.

/File Combine

Purpose

Combines values or formulas from a file or worksheet on disk into the current file.

Reminder

Use /FC to copy the contents from the file on disk to the current file, to add values from the file on disk to the current file, and to subtract incoming values from the numeric values in the current file.

To combine values or formulas

Type **/FC**. Then select **C**opy, **A**dd, or **S**ubtract. Select how much of the saved worksheet file you want to use. Choices include **E**ntire-File or **N**amed/Specified-Range.

If you select **N**amed/Specified-Range, you are asked to enter the range name (or the range address). If you select **E**ntire-File, choose a file name. Press **Enter**.

/File Dir

Purpose

Changes the current disk drive or directory for the current work session.

To change the current disk drive or directory

Type /FD. If the displayed drive and directory are correct, press Enter. To change the settings, type a new drive letter and directory name and press Enter.

/File Erase

Purpose

Erases 1-2-3 files from disk so that you have more available disk space.

Reminder

You cannot restore an erased file. Be sure that you will not need a file before you erase it.

To erase files

1. Type /FE.

2. Select the type of file you want to erase. Choices include Worksheet, Print, Graph, and Other.

3. Type the path and the name of the file, or use the arrow keys to highlight the file you want to erase. Press Enter.

4. Verify that you do or do not want to erase the file by selecting Yes or No from the menu.

/File Import

Purpose

Brings ASCII text files into 1-2-3 worksheets.

Reminder

Remember that /FI can be used in two ways to transfer data into a 1-2-3 worksheet. The first method reads each row of ASCII characters as left-aligned labels in a column; the second method reads into separate cells text enclosed in quotation marks or numbers surrounded by spaces or separated by commas.

To import ASCII files

1. Move the cell pointer to the upper left corner of the range in which you want to import data.

2. Type **/FI**.

3. Choose how to import the ASCII file. Choices include **T**ext and **N**umbers.

4. Select the ASCII print file. Press **Enter**.

/File List

Purpose

Displays all file names of a specific type that are stored on the current drive and directory. Displays the size of the file (in bytes) and the date and time the file was created.

To see a list of files

1. Type **/FL**.

2. Select the type of file you want to display. Choices include **W**orksheet, **P**rint, **G**raph, **O**ther, **A**ctive, and **L**inked.

3. Use the arrow keys to highlight individual file names and to display specific information.

4. Display files from a different directory by moving the cursor to a directory name and pressing **Enter**. Press **Backspace** to move to a parent directory.

5. Press **Enter** to return to the worksheet.

/File New

Purpose

Creates a new blank file on disk and positions a new worksheet on-screen before or after the current file.

To create a new file

1. Move the cell pointer to the file that will be adjacent to the new file's location.
2. Type **/FN**.
3. Choose the location for the new file. Choices include **B**efore and **A**fter.
4. Type a new file name to replace the default name given by 1-2-3. Press **Enter**.

/File Open

Purpose

Opens a file from disk into memory without removing active files.

To open a file

Type **/FO**. Then choose the location for the opening file. Choices include **B**efore and **A**fter. Specify the name of the file.

/File Retrieve

Purpose

Loads the requested worksheet file from disk.

Reminder

The retrieved file replaces the current file. Use **/F**ile **S**ave to store a current file before you retrieve a new file.

To retrieve a worksheet file

Type **/FR**. Select the file name you want to retrieve and press **Enter**.

/File Save

Purpose

Saves the current file or all active files and settings.

To save a file

1. Place the cell pointer in the active file you want to save.

2. Type **/FS**.

3. If more than one file is active, you get the message [ALL MODIFIED FILES]. To save all files, press **Enter**. To save only the current file, press **F2** or **Esc**, and the current file name is displayed.

4. If the file has not been saved previously, 1-2-3 supplies a default name and the extension (**FILE0001.WK3**, for example). You can enter the file name for the worksheet by using the default name displayed; by using → or ← to highlight an existing name; by typing a new name; or by entering a new drive designation, path name, and file name. Press **Enter**.

5. If there is an existing file with the name you have selected, choose **B**ackup, **C**ancel, or **R**eplace.

Choosing **R**eplace replaces the existing file on disk with the active file you are saving. You cannot recover the replaced file. Use **B**ackup to save a copy of the original file.

To save a file with a password

1. Place the cell pointer in the file you want to save.

2. Type **/FS**.

3. Type the file name, press the **space bar**, and type **P**. If [ALL MODIFIED FILES] is displayed, press **F2** to see the file name. Press **Enter**.

4. Type a password of up to 15 characters (no spaces). An asterisk appears for each letter. Memorize the upper- and lowercase letter combination. You must enter the exact password. Press **Enter**.

5. After the Verify prompt, type the password again and press **Enter**.

/File Xtract

Purpose

Saves to disk a portion of the active file as a separate file.

Reminders

You can save the portion as it appears on the worksheet (with formulas) or save only the results of the formulas.

Extracted ranges that include formulas must include the cells to which the formulas refer, or the formulas will be incorrect.

If CALC appears at the bottom of the screen, calculate the file by pressing **F9** before extracting values.

To save to disk a portion of a file

1. Position the cursor at the upper left corner of the range you want to extract.

2. Type **/FX**.

3. Choose **F**ormulas or **V**alues.

4. Type a file name other than the current file.

5. Specify the range of the file to be extracted as a separate file. Press **Enter**.

6. If the name already exists, choose **B**ackup, **C**ancel, or **R**eplace.

/Graph X/A/B/C/D/E/F

Purpose

Specifies the worksheet ranges containing x-axis and y-axis data or labels.

To specify the ranges containing x-axis and y-axis data

1. Type /G.

2. Select the ranges for x- or y-axis data or labels to be entered from these options:

Menu Item	Function
X	Enters x-axis label range. These are labels such as Jan, Feb, Mar, and so on. Creates labels for pie graph wedges and line, bar, and stacked-bar graphs.
A	Enters first y-axis data range. The only data range used by a pie graph.
B	Enters second y-axis data range. Enters pie graph shading values and extraction codes.
C	Enters third y-axis data range. Enters pie graph control over percentage labels.
D–F	Enters fourth through sixth data ranges.

3. Indicate the data range by entering the range address, using a range name, or highlighting the range.

4. Press Enter.

/Graph Group

Purpose

Quickly selects the data ranges for a graph, X and A through F, when data in adjacent rows and columns are in consecutive order.

To select a data range for a graph

1. Type /GG.

2. Specify the range containing X and A through F data values. The rows or columns must be adjacent and in the order X, A, B, C, D, E, and F.

3. Select Columnwise if the data ranges are in columns or Rowwise if the data ranges are in rows.

/Graph Name

Purpose

Stores graph settings for later use with the same worksheet.

Reminders

If you want to name a graph, make sure it is the active graph before naming it.

You can recall graphs in later work sessions only if you have saved the graph settings with /Graph Name Create and then saved the worksheet with /File Save.

Note that /Graph Name Reset deletes all graph names in the current worksheet and all graph parameters.

To create or modify a graph name

Type /GN. Then select one of the following options to name your file: Use, Create, Delete, Reset, or Table.

If you are switching to a new graph, creating a name, deleting or resetting names, specify the name. If you are creating a table of graph names, specify the location for the graph.

/Graph Options Advanced Colors

Purpose

Selects the colors used by data ranges A through F. The command can also be used to hide data ranges.

Reminder

/GOAC affects both the displayed and printed graph.

To select colors for a data range

1. Type **/GOAC**.

2. Select the data range you want to change, **A** through **F**.

3. Select the appearance of that data range:

Menu Item	Function
1–8	Colors 1 through 8 are set for the entire data range, A–F.
Hide	Hides this data range.
Range	Specifies colors for specific data items within the range A–F. Colors are entered as numbers, 1 through 14, in a range that matches the size of the range to which the colors have been assigned.

4. If you selected **R**ange, specify the range containing the colors.

/Graph Options Advanced Hatches

Purpose

Changes the hatching (shading) for each data range in a graph.

Reminder

/GOAH affects the displayed and the printed graph.

To add hatching to a data range

1. Type **/GOAH**.
2. Specify the range you want to hatch.
3. Select the hatch pattern:

Menu Item	*Function*
1–8	Uses the hatch pattern that corresponds to the number chosen.
Range	Specifies hatch patterns for specific data items within the range A through F. Hatch patterns are entered as numbers, 1 through 14, in a range the same size as the range to which the hatch patterns are assigned.

   If you are using **R**ange, specify the range containing the hatch values.

/Graph Options Advanced Text

Purpose

Changes the font, size, and color for graph text.

Reminder

/GOAT affects the displayed and the printed graph.

To modify graph text

1. Type /GOA.
2. Select Text.
3. Select the group of text you want to change: First, Second, or Third.
4. Select Color.
5. Select the color for the group of text you want to change. Options are 1 through 8 or Hide.
6. Select Font.
7. Select the font you want for the group of text. Options are 1 through 8 or Default.
8. Select Size.
9. Select the size of font you want for the group of text. Sizes are 1 through 9 and Default.

/Graph Options Color/B&W

Purpose

Defines the colors 1-2-3 uses to display graphs on your monitor.

To define colors

To set the color option, type /GOC.

To set the black and white option, type /GOB.

Note

Color monitors that are set to /GOC, but have printers with only black-and-white capabilities, will print black and white. To set color text, use /Graph Options Advanced Text Color. To set color shading, use /Graph Options Advanced Colors.

/Graph Options Data-Labels

Purpose

Labels graph points from data contained in cells.

To assign data labels

1. Type /GOD.

2. Select the data range to which you want to assign labels. Choices include A–F, Group, and Quit.

3. Specify the range containing the labels. This range should be the same size as the range you selected for A through F. If you are grouping data ranges, the range selected must be the same size as all the data ranges combined.

4. Select the data label location relative to the corresponding data points from the following options: Center, Left, Above, Right, and Below.

/Graph Options Format

Purpose

Selects the symbols and lines that identify and connect data points.

Some line and XY graphs present information more clearly if the data is displayed only as data points; other graphs present information better if the data is represented by a series of data points linked with a solid line. Use /Graph Options Format to select the type of data points used for each data range (symbols, lines, or both).

To format graph options

1. Type /GOF.

2. Select Graph or A–F to define the data ranges to be formatted.

3. Select the data point type: Lines, Symbols, Both, Neither, and Area.

/Graph Options Grid

Purpose

Overlays a grid on a graph to enhance readability.

To overlay a grid on a graph

Type /GOG. Then select the type of grid. Choices include Horizontal, Vertical, Both, Clear, and Y-axis.

/Graph Options Legend

Purpose

Indicates which line, bar, or point belongs to a specific y-axis data range.

Reminder

Y-axis data and legend titles for each range are entered in ranges A, B, C, D, E, and F. If, by using /Move, /Worksheet Insert, or /Worksheet Delete, you relocate a graph, 1-2-3 will not adjust cell addresses that have been used to create legends. Use range names to describe legend ranges.

To specify a graph legend

1. Type /GOL.

2. Select A–F or Range.

3. If you choose A through F, enter the text for the legend. If you choose Range, specify the range containing the legends.

/Graph Options Scale

Purpose

Varies the scale along either y-axes. The x-axis scale can be varied on XY-type graphs.

Reminders

Options within the command include:

- Making changes manually to the upper- or lower-axis end points.

- Choosing formats for numeric display. (Options are identical to those in /Worksheet Global Format or /Range Format.)

- Improving display of overlapping x-axis labels by skipping every specified occurrence, such as every second or third label.

To modify a graph scale

1. Type /GOS.

2. Select the axis or skip frequency to be changed. Choices include Y-Scale, X-Scale, Skip, and 2Y-Scale.

3. If you select the Y-Scale, 2Y-Scale, or X-Scale menu items, select the menu item to be scaled. Choices include Automatic, Manual, Lower, Upper, Format, Indicator, Type, Exponent, Width, and Quit.

4. If you choose Skip, enter a number to indicate the frequency intervals at which the x-axis scale tick marks will appear.

/Graph Options Titles

Purpose

Adds headings to the graph and to each axis.

To add titles to a graph

Type **/GOT**. Then select **F**irst, **S**econd, **X**-Axis, **Y**-Axis, **2**Y-Axis, **N**ote, or **O**ther Note to define the title to be entered. Enter a title, cell address, or range name of a cell containing a title.

/Graph Reset

Purpose

Cancels all or some of a graph's setting so that you can create a new graph or exclude one or more data ranges.

To cancel graph settings

Type **/GR**. Then choose **G**raph, **X**, **A**–**F**, **R**anges, **O**ptions, or **Q**uit.

/Graph Save

Purpose

Enables the graph to be modified by a different program.

To save a graph

Type **/GS**. Then specify a file name and press **Enter**.

/Graph Type

Purpose

Selects from among the 1-2-3 graph types, according to which type of graph is best suited for displaying data.

To select a graph type

1. Type **/GT**.

2. Select the type of graph:

Menu Item	Function
Line	Usually depicts a continuous series of data. Line graphs can be altered to appear as area graphs.
Bar	Usually displays distinctly separate data series.
XY	Graphs data sets of x and y data; XY graphs have data on both axes.
Stack-Bar	Shows how proportions change within the whole.
Pie	Shows how the whole is divided into component portions. Use only the A range to contain the values of each portion. The X range is used to label the pie wedges.
HLCO	Tracks items that vary over time. Most commonly used in the stock market to show the price at which a stock opens and closes and its high and low prices during the day.
Mixed	Contains bar and line graphs. Relates trends in two distinct measurable quantities. If the scales for items vary significantly, a second y-axis (2Y Axis) can be added with a different scale. Mixed graphs can have up to three bars and three lines.
Features	Provides additional choices:
	Vertical orients the graph vertically (default selection).
	Horizontal rotates the graph so that the y-axis is horizontal and the x-axis is vertical.

Stacked stacks ranges on top of each other.

100% stacks ranges on top of each other as a percentage of the total. All stacks equal 100%.

2 Y-Ranges assigns ranges to a second y-scale on the right side of the graph.

Y-Ranges assigns ranges to a first y-scale on the left side of the graph; the default.

3. The **G**raph menu reappears.

/Graph View

Purpose

Displays a graph on-screen.

Reminder

Your system hardware and system configuration determines what is displayed on-screen.

To display a graph

Type **/GV**. Then press any key to return to the **G**raph menu.

/Move

Purpose

Moves ranges of labels, values, or formulas to different locations or worksheets.

To move data

1. Type **/M**.

1-2-3 Command Reference

2. The FROM: prompt requests the range of the cells to be moved. Highlight a range or type the range name or the range address. Press Enter.

3. At the TO: prompt, enter the address of the single upper left corner of the range to which the cells will be moved. Press Enter.

/Print

Purpose

Initiates the main print menus.

To operate the main print menu

Type /P. Then select the /Print command. Choices include Printer, File, Encoded, Suspend, Resume, Cancel, and Quit.

Throughout the following /Print commands, the individual File/Encoded options may not be listed in the headers. The available menu options will, however, be listed directly under each header.

For example, the header "/Print Printer Options Margins" followed by "/PPOM or /PFOM or /PEOM" indicates that in addition to /Print Printer, you can select /Print File or /Print Encoded.

/Print Printer/File/Encoded

Purpose

Prints worksheet contents and graphs.

/PP prints directly to the printer. /PF prints worksheet contents as an ASCII text file to disk so that you may import the file into other programs. /PE prints a print-image file to disk so that you may print it later.

Reminder

When you select /PP, /PF, or /PE, you get the main print menu. All print settings apply equally to all three options. If you select /PF and specify a **R**ange, for example, the next time you select /PP (or /PE), 1-2-3 remembers the **R**ange selected with /PF.

To print a range to a printer

1. Type **/PP**, **/PF**, or **/PE**.

2. For /PF or /PE, enter the print file name. With /PF, 1-2-3 automatically gives the file name a PRN extension. With /PE, 1-2-3 automatically gives the file name an ENC extension.

3. Select **R**ange.

4. Specify the range or ranges to be printed.

5. Select other options as needed.

6. Select **G**o to print the range(s).

/Print Printer Align

Purpose

Aligns 1-2-3's internal line counter to the top of a physical page in the printer.

Resets the page number to 1.

Reminder

Use this command only when the paper is at the top of a new page.

To synchronize 1-2-3 with the printer

If necessary, position the printer paper so that the top of a page is aligned with the printhead. Type **/PP**, **/PF**, or **/PE**. Then select **A**lign to synchronize 1-2-3 with the printer.

/Print Printer Clear

Purpose

Clears some or all print settings and options.

Reminders

Cleared formats return to default settings.

This option is the only way to clear borders after they have been set.

Print parameters remain in effect until you issue different instructions. To issue a new set of parameters, use **/P**rint **P**rinter **C**lear **A**ll.

To clear print settings

Type **/PPC**, **/PFC**, or **/PEC**. Then select **A**ll, **R**anges, **B**orders, **F**ormat, **I**mage, or **D**evice.

/Print Printer Hold

Purpose

Permits you to return to READY mode with the print job open.

To leave a print job after you have issued /PP, /PF, or /PE

Select **H**old.

To take a print job off hold

Do one of the following:

- Return to the main **P**rint menu and complete the job.
- Select **/P**rint **C**ancel.
- Select a different printer or printer interface.
- Select a different type of printing (Printer, File, or Encoded).

/Print Printer Image

Purpose

Selects the graph you want to print.

Reminder

If 1-2-3 does not have enough memory available to print the graph when requested, save and delete files from memory. Use /Print Resume to resume printing.

To select a graph to print

1. Type /PP or /PE.
2. Select Image.
3. Select Current or Named-Graph.
4. If you select Named-Graph, specify the name of the graph you want to print.
5. Select Options Advanced Image to format the appearance of the graph on the page.

/Print Printer Line

Purpose

Advances printer paper by one line.

To advance the printer page by one line

Type /PP, /PF, or /PE. Then select Line to advance the paper by one line. Repeat the keystroke (or press Enter) as many times as necessary to advance the paper.

/Print Printer Options Advanced

Purpose

Uses the full printing capabilities of your printer to enhance printing and graphs.

Reminder

Use **/P**rint **S**ample before you select fonts to check the capabilities of your printer.

To enhance printing and graphs

Type **/PPOA** or **/PEOA**. Then select one of the following commands:

Menu Item	*Function*
Device	Selects the printer to which you want to print with the **N**ame command and the printer interface with the **I**nterface command.
Layout	Selects printer characteristics that affect character and line spacing. These characteristics may vary with your printer and include the following settings:

Pitch lets you choose the number of characters per inch (cpi).

Standard is approximately 10 cpi; **C**ompressed is 17 cpi; **E**xpanded is 5 cpi.

Line-Spacing sets the line spacing on your page. **S**tandard is 6 lines per inch; **C**ompressed is 8 lines per inch.

Menu Item	Function
	Orientation sets the direction in which printed characters appear on a page. **P**ortrait is normal or vertical on the page. **L**andscape is sideways or horizontal on the page.
Fonts	Selects different typefaces and styles for a print range. Font settings include the following:
	Range highlights the worksheet range you want to change, then selects a font from 1 to 8.
	Header/Footer selects a font from 1 to 8 for both the header and footer.
	Border selects a font from 1 to 8 for the border.
	Frame selects a font from 1 to 8 for the frame.
Color	Selects the color in which you want to print text. All text prints in the same color. Select a color from 1 to 8.
Image	Selects the quality, size, and orientation of printed graphs. Image settings include the following:
	Rotate changes the orientation of the graph with the text. Choose **Y**es if you want the graph rotated; choose **N**o to keep the graph oriented with the text.
	Image-Size sets the size and shape of the graph. **L**ength-Fill creates the maximum-sized graph within the length you enter. **M**argin-Fill creates

1-2-3 Command Reference

the maximum-sized graph within the width you enter. **R**eshape creates a graph in the dimensions you enter. **L**ength-Fill and **M**argin-Fill preserve proportions.

Density prints in **F**inal for high-quality graphs; **D**raft prints graphs faster, but at a lower print quality.

Priority — Selects the priority for the current print job with respect to other jobs. Priority settings include the following:

Default prints the current job after other jobs, but before **L**ow priority jobs.

Low prints the current job after all other jobs.

High prints the current job ahead of the **D**efault and **L**ow priority jobs.

AutoLf — Selects the opposite of current setting. Used when the chosen printer uses a different line-feed setting from the default printer, if lines print on top of each other, or if they double-space.

Wait — Suspends printing after ejecting a page so that you can insert a new page. Use **/P**rint **R**esume to continue after inserting a page.

Note

If you select COM1 or COM2 as the printer interface, you must use your operating system's MODE command to configure this printer port.

/Print Printer Options Borders

Purpose

Prints on every page the rows or columns selected from the worksheet.

Reminder

If you include in the print range the rows or columns specified as borders, they will be printed twice.

To print rows or columns on every page

1. Type **/PPOB**, **/PFOB**, or **/PEOB**.

2. Select **C**olumns or **R**ows.

3. Press **Esc** to remove the current range. Specify the borders range. Press **Enter**.

/Print Printer Options Footer/Header

Purpose

Prints a footer above the bottom margin or a header above the top margin of each page.

To print a footer or header

Type **/PPO**, **/PFO**, or **/PEO**. Then select **F**ooter or **H**eader. You can type a footer or header as wide as the margin and paper widths. Press **Enter**.

Notes

Use headers and footers for titles, dates, and page numbers.

To print the date and page number automatically in the footer or header, enter an at sign (@) where you want the date to appear and a number sign (#) where you want the page number to appear.

Use ## followed by a number to start the page numbering at that number. Type ##6 to show the first page as page 6, for example.

Use \ followed by a cell address to insert the contents of a cell into the header or footer.

Separate the footer or header into as many as three centered segments by entering a vertical bar (|). To print in three segments with a system date of October 25, 1989, at page 21, for example, enter:

@|Hill and Dale|Page #

This prints as:

```
25-Oct-89        Hill and Dale        Page 21
```

To center the data, place one vertical bar to the left of the data. To left-justify the data, do not include vertical bars. To right-justify the data, insert two vertical bars.

To right-justify the page number, for example, enter:

||Page #

/Print Printer Options Margins

Purpose

Changes the left, right, top, and bottom margins.

To set margins for printing

Type **/PPOM**, **/PFOM**, or **/PEOM**. Then specify margins. Choices include **L**eft, **R**ight, **T**op, **B**ottom, and **N**one.

/Print Printer Options Name

Purpose

Assigns names to print settings used frequently.

Helps you manage your library of print setting names.

To name print settings

1. Type **/PPO**, **/PFO**, or **/PEO**.
2. Select **N**ame **C**reate.
3. Type a name for the settings of 15 characters or less. Do not use an opening chevron (<<). Using an existing name will replace the settings for that name with the new settings.

To change settings assigned to an existing name

1. Type **/PPO**, **/PFO**, or **/PEO**.
2. Select **N**ame **U**se.
3. Select the name you want to modify.
4. Change settings using **/P**rint commands.
5. Type **/PPONC**, **/PFONC**, or **/PEONC**.
6. Select the same name you selected in Step 3.

To delete a print setting name

1. Type **/PPO**, **/PFO**, or **/PEO**.
2. Select **N**ame **D**elete.
3. Select the name you want to delete.

To delete all print setting names in a file

1. Make sure that the cell pointer is in the file from which you want to delete names.
2. Type **/PPO**, **/PFO**, or **/PEO**.
3. Select **N**ame **R**eset.

To create a table containing a list of all the print setting names

1. Move the cell pointer to a blank area in the current worksheet that is one column wide and as many rows long as there are print setting names.
2. Type **/PPO**, **/PFO**, or **/PEO**.
3. Select **N**ame **T**able and press **Enter**.

/Print Printer Options Other

Purpose

Selects the form and formatting in which cells print.

To select the format in which cells print

Type **/PPOO**, **/PFOO**, or **/PEOO**. Then select the printing method. Choices include **A**s-Displayed, **C**ell-Formulas, **F**ormatted, **U**nformatted, and **B**lank-Header.

/Print Printer Options Pg-Length

Purpose

Specifies the number of lines per page using a standard 6-lines-per-inch page height.

To specify the number of lines per page

Type **/PPOP**, **/PFOP**, or **/PEOP**. Then enter the number of lines per page if that number is different from the number shown. Page length can be from 1 to 1,000 lines. Press **Enter**.

/Print Printer Options Setup

Purpose

Sends formatting commands to the printer.

Reminders

Before using setup strings, check the **/P**rint [**P**rinter, **E**ncoded] **O**ptions **A**dvanced commands to see if an equivalent command is available.

Do not combine setup strings with the menu commands for the same feature. The result is unpredictable.

Your printer manual lists printer control codes or escape codes.

To send formatting codes to the printer

1. Type **/PPOS** or **/PEOS**.

2. Enter the setup string. If a setup string has already been entered, press **Esc** to clear the string. Each control code must begin with a backslash (\). Upper- or lowercase letters must be typed as shown in your printer's manual.

3. Press **Enter**.

Note

1-2-3 setup strings include decimal number codes (three-digit numbers), preceded by a backslash (\). If the EPSON printer control code for condensed print, for example, is 15, then the 1-2-3 setup string is **\015**. Setup strings can hold up to 512 characters.

/Print Printer Page

Purpose

Controls paper feed by moving the paper to the bottom of the page for printing any footer, and then by advancing the paper until the printhead is at the top of the next page.

To control paper feed

Type **/PP**, **/PF**, or **/PE**. Then select **P**age to print any footer at the bottom of the page, and to position the printhead at the top of the next page.

/Print Printer Range

Purpose

Defines the area of the worksheet to be printed.

To define the area to print

1. Type **/PPR**, **/PFR**, or **/PER**.

2. Specify the range to be printed: type the range address, highlight the range, or enter an assigned range name.

3. To print multiple ranges, separate each range with a comma or semicolon.

4. Press **Enter**.

/Print Printer Sample

Purpose

Prints a sample page from the printer, showing the capabilities of your printer.

To print a sample page

Type **/PP**, **/PF**, or **/PE**. Then select **S**ample and then **A**lign **G**o.

/Quit

Purpose

Exits 1-2-3 and returns to the operating system.

Reminder

Files that are not saved with **/F**ile **S**ave are lost when you exit 1-2-3.

To exit 1-2-3

1. Type **/Q**.

2. Select **Y**es to quit 1-2-3 and return to the operating system. Select **N**o to return to 1-2-3 and the current worksheet.

3. Select **Y**es to quit without saving (abandon the changes) if you made changes to the worksheet. Select **N**o to return to the worksheet.

4. If you started 1-2-3 from the Access System Menu, you will return to it. Choose **E**xit from the Access System menu to leave it. If you started 1-2-3 by typing **123**, you will return to the operating system.

See also File Save and File Xtract.

/Range Erase

Purpose

Erases the contents of a single cell or a range of cells, but leaves the cell's format intact.

To erase the contents of a range

Type **/RE**. Then specify the range to be erased. Press **Enter**.

/Range Format

Purpose

Prepares cells so that they are displayed with a specific format.

Reminders

Range formats take precedence over Worksheet Global formats.

/RF rounds only the appearance of the displayed number; it does not round the number used for calculation. As a result, displayed or printed numbers may appear to be incorrect answers to formulas. Use @ROUND to ensure that the values in calculations are rounded properly.

1-2-3 Command Reference

To format a range

1. Type **/RF**.
2. Select a format from the following menu items:

Menu Item	Function
Fixed	Sets the number of decimal places displayed.
Scientific	Displays large or small numbers, using scientific notation.
Currency	Displays currency symbols ($, for example) and commas.
,	Inserts commas to mark thousands and multiples of thousands.
General	Displays values with no special formatting.
+/–	Creates horizontal bar graphs. Each symbol is equal to one whole number. Positive numbers are displayed as plus (+) symbols; negative numbers are displayed as minus (–) symbols.
Percent	Displays a decimal number as a whole percentage with a % sign.
Date	Displays serial-date numbers in the following formats. Select the corresponding number for formats.

1 DD-MMM-YY		12-Jan-89
2 DD-MMM		12-Jan
3 MMM-YY		Jan-89
4 MM/DD/YY		01/12/89
5 MM/DD		01/12

Menu Item	Function
Time	Displays time factions.
Text	Continues to evaluate formulas as numbers, but displays formulas as text on-screen.
Hidden	Hides contents from the display and does not print them, but still evaluates contents.
Other	Enables additional formatting options, including the following:

Automatic formats numbers and dates as they are entered.

There are two choices for **C**olor: **N**egative displays negative numbers in color; **R**eset turns off color formats.

Label formats all entries as labels using a label prefix.

There are two choices for **P**arenthesis: **Y**es encloses all numbers in parentheses; **N**o removes parentheses.

Reset	Returns the format to current **/W**orksheet **G**lobal format.

3. Enter the number of decimal places to be displayed if 1-2-3 prompts you to do so. The full value of a cell is used for calculation, not the value displayed.

4. Specify the range by entering the range address, highlighting the range, or using an assigned range name. Press **Enter**.

Note

To apply a format to the same cells in all worksheets in the file, put the file in GROUP mode with **/W**orksheet **G**lobal **G**roup and perform a range format.

/Range Input

Purpose

Enables cell-pointer movement in unprotected cells only.

Reminders

To use **/R**ange **I**nput effectively, organize your worksheet so that the data-entry cells are together.

Before you use /RI, use **/R**ange **U**nprotect to identify unprotected data entry cells. You do not have to enable **/W**orksheet **G**lobal **P**rot to use /RI.

To restrict cell-pointer movement to unprotected cells

1. Type **/RI**.

2. Specify the input range. Include a range that covers all cells in which you want to display or enter data.

3. Press **Enter**. The input range's upper left corner is moved to the screen's upper left corner. Cell-pointer movement is restricted to unprotected cells in the designated input range.

4. Make data entries, using normal methods. Press **Esc** or **Enter** to exit **/R**ange **I**nput.

/Range Justify

Purpose

Fits text within a desired range by wrapping words to form complete paragraphs and redistributes words so that text lines are approximately the same length.

To justify text

1. Type **/RJ**.

2. Highlight the range in which you want the text to be justified. If you do not specify a range, highlight only the first row of the text column.

/Range Label

Purpose

Selects how you want to align text labels in their cells.

To align text labels

1. Type **/RL**.

2. Select **L**eft, **R**ight, or **C**enter.

3. Specify the range by entering the range address, highlighting the range, or using an assigned range name. Press **Enter**.

/Range Name

Purpose

Assigns a name to a cell or a range of cells.

Reminder

Moving one or more corners of a range can redefine the range name. Check the addresses to which a range name applies by issuing **/R**ange **N**ame **C**reate and selecting the name in question. Its range is displayed on-screen. Press **Ctrl-Break** or **Esc** to return to the menu.

To create a range name

1. Type **/RN**.

2. Select **C**reate.

3. Type a range name consisting of up to 15 characters. Avoid using symbols other than the underline and backslash. Press **Enter**.

4. Specify the range to be named. Press **Enter**.

1-2-3 Command Reference

To create range names from labels
1. Type **/RN**.
2. Select **L**abels.
3. Select **R**ight, **D**own, **L**eft, or **U**p.
4. Specify the range of labels to be used as range names for adjacent cells by entering the range address or highlighting the range. Press **Enter**.

To delete one or more range names
1. Type **/RN**.
2. Select **D**elete to delete a single range name. Select **R**eset to delete all range names.
3. If you select **D**elete, type or highlight the name you want to delete and press **Enter**. Formulas containing the range names will now use cell and range addresses.

To create a table of existing range names and addresses
Type **/RN**. Then select **T**able and press **Enter**.

To attach or edit notes associated with a range name
1. Type **/RN**.
2. Choose **N**ote **C**reate.
3. Specify the range address to which you want to attach a note. Press **Enter**.
4. Type or edit a note of up to 512 characters and press **Enter**.

To delete one or more notes associated with range names
1. Type **/RN**.
2. Choose **N**ote **D**elete to delete one range name note or **N**ote **R**eset to delete all range name notes.
3. If you choose **N**ote **D**elete, specify the range name of the note you want to delete.

To display a table of range name notes in the current file
Type **/RN**. Then choose **N**ote **T**able and press **Enter**.

Notes

Instead of cell addresses, use range names to make formulas and macros easy to read and understand.

Use a range name when you enter a function. Instead of entering a function as **@SUM(P53..P65)**, for example, type it as **@SUM(EXPENSES)**.

Use a range name when you respond to a prompt. When the program requests a print range, for example, provide a range name, as in the following example:

Enter print range: **JULREPORT**.

/Range Prot/Unprot

Purpose

Changes the protection status of a range.

Use /RP, /RU, and **/W**orksheet **G**lobal **P**rot to protect worksheets from accidental changes. /RU identifies which cell contents can be changed when **/W**orksheet **G**lobal **P**rot is used.

To unprotect a cell or a range of cells

Type **/RU**. Then specify the range and press **Enter**.

To remove the unprotected status from a range

Type **/RP**. Then specify the range and press **Enter**.

Notes

/Range **P**rot and **/R**ange **U**nprot affect data entry only when **/W**orksheet **G**lobal **P**rot is enabled.

On some displays, the contents of unprotected cells increase in intensity or change color.

When the file is in GROUP mode and you identify a range as unprotected on one worksheet, the same range is identified and unprotected on all worksheets.

/Range Search

Purpose
Finds or replaces text within a range. Searches and replaces can be limited to labels or formulas.

Reminder
You cannot use /RS to find or replace numbers.

To find or replace text
1. Type /RS.
2. Specify the range you want to search.
3. Enter the text string you want to find or replace. Either upper- or lowercase text may be used.
4. Choose Formulas, Labels, or Both.
5. Choose Find or Replace.
6. If you choose Find, 1-2-3 will find and display the cell that contains the specified text. Choose Next to find other occurrences, or choose Quit to stop the search.

   If you choose Replace, type the replacement string, press Enter, and 1-2-3 finds and displays the cell that contains the specified text. You should then choose Replace, All, Next, or Quit.

/Range Trans

Purpose
Copies formulas from one location and orientation to another location and orientation. Formulas are replaced by values.

Transposes data from rows and columns on one worksheet to rows or columns on multiple worksheets.

Reminder

Make sure that the source file is calculated. If CALC is displayed at the bottom of the screen, press F9 to recalculate the file.

To transpose data

1. Type /RT.

2. Specify the range to be transposed. Press Enter.

3. If you want to transpose rows with columns or columns with rows on a single worksheet, specify the upper left corner of the area where you want the transposed data to appear.

   If you want to transpose data across multiple worksheets, specify the upper left corner of the three-dimensional range for each copy on each of the multiple worksheets. Move the cell pointer to the upper left corner of the destination cells to where the transposed data will be copied.

4. Press Enter. The data will transpose immediately if you are working on a single worksheet.

5. If you are transposing across multiple worksheets, choose one of the following commands:

Menu Item	Function
Rows/Columns	Copies rows to columns or vice versa.
Worksheets/Rows	Copies each row to a succeeding worksheet in the TO: range.
Columns/Worksheets	Copies each column to a succeeding worksheet in the TO: range.

/Range Value

Purpose

Replaces formulas in the same or new location with their resulting values.

1-2-3 Command Reference

Copies labels and string formulas and converts string (text) formulas to labels.

Reminder

Make sure that the source file is calculated. If CALC appears at the bottom of the screen, press **F9** to recalculate the file.

To replace formulas with values

1. Type **/RV**.
2. Specify the source range. Press **Enter**.
3. Specify the upper left corner cell of the destination range.
4. Press **Enter**. The values appear in the destination range. These values preserve the numeric formats used in the original formulas.

/System

Purpose

Exits 1-2-3 temporarily so that you can run DOS commands or other programs, and returns to 1-2-3 and the worksheet on which you were working.

Reminder

Be certain that the programs you run from 1-2-3 will fit in your computer's available memory. Do not load or run memory-resident programs while in System.

To exit 1-2-3 temporarily

1. Type **/S**.
2. Type the DOS commands or programs.
3. When you finish running a program, return to DOS.
4. To return to 1-2-3 from the DOS prompt, type **EXIT** and press **Enter**.

/Worksheet Column

Purpose

Adjusts the column width of one or more columns.

To adjust column width

1. Type /WC.

2. Select Set-Width, Reset-Width, Hide, Display, or Column-Range.

3. If you choose Set-Width, enter the new column width by typing the number of characters, or by pressing ← or → to shrink or expand the column.

   If you choose Hide or Display, indicate which columns you want to change.

   If you choose Column-Range, choose Set-Width or Reset-Width, indicate the columns you want to change, enter the column width as a number, or press ← or → to shrink or expand the column. Press Enter.

/Worksheet Delete

Purpose

Deletes one or more columns or rows from the worksheet. Deletes one or more worksheets from a file or deletes an active file from memory but not from the disk.

To delete columns, rows, worksheets, or files

Type /WD. Then select Column, Row, Sheet, or File. Specify a range containing the columns, rows, or worksheets you want to delete. If you want to delete a file, specify the file.

/Worksheet Erase

Purpose

Erases all active files from memory, leaving one blank worksheet on-screen and in memory.

Reminder

Be sure to save active files before you use **/W**orksheet **E**rase.

To erase all active files from memory

Type **/WE**. Then select **Y**es or **N**o.

/Worksheet Global Col-Width

Purpose

Sets column width for the entire worksheet. If GROUP mode is on, sets column width for the entire file.

To set the global worksheet column width

Type **/WGC**. Then enter a number for the column width used most frequently, or press → to increase column width or ← to decrease column width. Press **Enter**.

/Worksheet Global Default

Purpose

Specifies display formats and start-up settings for hardware.

Used to control how 1-2-3 works with the printer, which disk and directory are accessed automatically, which international displays are used, and which type of clock is displayed.

To specify worksheet default settings

1. Type **/WGD**.
2. Select the setting you want to change:

Menu Item	Function
Printer	Specifies printer settings and connections. Choose from the following options:
	Interface selects parallel or serial port.
	Auto-LF instructs 1-2-3 to insert a line feed automatically after each printer line.
	Left Margin (default is 4, 0–1,000).
	Right Margin (default is 76, 0–1,000).
	Top Margin (default is 2, 0–240).
	Bottom Margin (default is 2, 0–240).
	Pg-Length (default is 66, 1–1,000).
	Wait pauses for page insert at the end of each page.
	Setup sets the initial printer-control codes.
	Name selects from multiple printers.
Dir	Specifies the directory for read or write operations. Press **Esc** to clear. Type the new directory; press **Enter**.
Status	Displays settings for **/W**orksheet **G**lobal **D**efault.
Update	Saves to disk the current global defaults for use with the next startup.

Other	**I**nternational specifies display settings for **P**unctuation, **C**urrency, **D**ate, **T**ime, **N**egative formats, **R**elease-2 character sets, and **F**ile-Translation for international characters.
	Help is always **R**emovable in Releases 3.1 and 3.1+, but is retained for compatibility with Release 2 macros.
	Clock displays **S**tandard or **I**nternational date and time formats or **N**one. Displays date and time (set by other commands), or displays the file name (set by **F**ilename).
	Undo enables or disables the Undo feature.
	Beep turns on or off the computer's sound.
Graph	Sets the directions used by 1-2-3 to divide cell ranges into graph ranges. Also specifies the graph file format when you save a graph.
Temp	Sets the directory where 1-2-3 saves temporary files used during operation.
Ext	**S**ave changes the file extensions with which files are saved. **L**ist changes the file extensions of files that are displayed by **/F**ile commands.
Autoexec	Enables or disables the capability to automatically run autoexecute macros.

/Worksheet Global Format

Purpose

Defines the default display format for numeric values and formulas in the worksheet.

In GROUP mode, defines the default display format for the entire file.

To define the default numeric format

1. Type **/WGF**.

2. Select **F**ixed, **S**cientific, **C**urrency, **G**eneral, **+/−**, **P**ercent, **D**ate, **T**ime, **T**ext, **H**idden, or **O**ther. See /Range Format for explanations of these choices.

3. After you select **F**ixed, **S**cientific, **C**urrency, comma (**,**), or **P**ercent, enter the number of decimal places. Press **Enter**. Numbers that are stored in the cells are accurate up to 19 digits to the right of the decimal. The stored numbers, not the displayed numbers, are used in calculations.

/Worksheet Global Group

Purpose

In GROUP mode, applies the format of one worksheet to all worksheets in the file.

To apply the format of one worksheet to all worksheets

Type **/WGG**. Then select **D**isable to turn off GROUP or **E**nable to turn on GROUP.

Notes

When GROUP is enabled, you will see the GROUP status indicator displayed at the bottom of the screen.

When in GROUP mode, the following commands affect all worksheets: **/R**ange [**F**ormat, **L**abel, **P**rot, **U**nprot], **/W**orksheet [**C**olumn, **D**elete **C**olumn/**R**ow, **I**nsert **C**olumn/**R**ow, **P**age, **T**itles], and **/W**orksheet **G**lobal [**C**ol-Width, **F**ormat, **L**abel, **P**rot, **Z**ero].

/Worksheet Global Label

Purpose

Selects text label alignment throughout the worksheet. When GROUP mode is on, changes the label alignment throughout the entire file.

To align label text globally

Type **/WGL**. Then select **L**eft, **R**ight, or **C**enter. Type the labels as you want them to appear on the worksheet.

See also /Worksheet Global Format, /Range Format, and /Range Label.

/Worksheet Global Prot

Purpose

Protects the worksheet or file from being changed. In GROUP mode, protects the entire file.

Reminders

Cells marked with **/R**ange **U**nprot will be unprotected when worksheet protection is on.

Before or after you protect the entire worksheet, you can use **/R**ange **U**nprot to specify cells that can be modified.

To protect a worksheet

Type **/WGP**. Then select one of these options:

Menu Item	Function
Enable	Protects the worksheet. Only cells specified with **/R**ange **U**nprot can be changed.
Disable	Removes protection from the worksheet. Any cell can be changed.

/Worksheet Global Recalc

Purpose

Defines how files recalculate and how many times they calculate.

To define how worksheets recalculate

1. Type **/WGR**.

2. Select one of the following:

Menu Item	*Function*
Natural	Calculates formulas that depend upon other formulas last.
Columnwise	Starts at the top of column A and recalculates downward, then moves to column B, recalculating downward, and so on.
Rowwise	Starts at the beginning of row 1 and recalculates to the end, then continues through proceeding rows.
Automatic	Recalculates when cell contents change.
Manual	Recalculates only when you press the F9 (Calc) key or when {CALC} is encountered in a macro. The CALC indicator appears at the bottom of the screen when recalculation is advised.
Iteration	Recalculates the worksheet a specified number of times.

3. If you select **I**teration, enter a number from **1** to **50**. The default setting is 1. **I**teration works with

Columnwise and Rowwise recalculations or with Natural recalculation when the worksheet contains a circular reference.

4. If you select Columnwise or Rowwise recalculation, you may need to repeat Step 1 and select Iteration in Step 2. In Step 3, enter the number of recalculations necessary for correct results. Columnwise and Rowwise recalculations often require multiple calculations to ensure that all worksheet results are correct.

/Worksheet Global Zero

Purpose

Suppresses zeros from appearing in displays and printed reports, or displays a label instead. Applies to the entire file when GROUP mode is on.

To suppress the display of zeros

1. Type /WGZ.

2. Choose from among the following commands:

Menu Item	Function
Yes	Suppresses the display of cells containing zero or a result of zero.
No	Displays cells containing zero or a result of zero as zero.
Label	Displays a label that you enter in place of zero or in place of zero as a result.

3. If you choose Label, enter the label you want to display and press Enter. Precede the label with an apostrophe (') for left alignment or a caret (^) for right alignment. Default label alignment is set at right alignment.

/Worksheet Hide

Purpose

Hides or displays one or more worksheets.

Reminder

Be careful not to delete hidden worksheets when deleting across a range of worksheets.

To hide or display a worksheet

1. Type **/WH**.

2. Select **E**nable to hide worksheets or **D**isable to display worksheets.

3. Specify the range containing the worksheets you want to hide or display. Press **Enter**.

/Worksheet Insert

Purpose

Inserts one or more blank columns or rows in the worksheet or one or more blank worksheets in the file.

Use this command to add space for formulas, data, or text, or to add worksheets to a file to create three-dimensional worksheets.

To insert columns, rows, or worksheets

1. Type **/WI**.

2. Select **C**olumn, **R**ow, or **W**orksheet.

3. If you choose **W**orksheet, select **B**efore or **A**fter to indicate whether you want to insert the new worksheets before or after the current worksheet. Indicate the number of worksheets you want to insert. The total number of worksheets in a file cannot exceed 256.

If you choose Column, move the cell pointer right to highlight one cell for each column you want to insert. If you choose Row, move the pointer down to highlight one cell for each row you want to insert.

4. Press Enter.

/Worksheet Page

Purpose

Manually inserts page breaks in printed worksheets. When GROUP mode is on, the page break is inserted in all worksheets in the file.

To insert page breaks

Type /WP. A row is inserted and a double colon (::) appears in the left column.

/Worksheet Status

Purpose

Displays the current global settings and hardware options. Also checks available memory.

To display the worksheet status

Type /WS. Then press any key to return to the worksheet.

/Worksheet Titles

Purpose

Displays column or row headings that might otherwise be scrolled off the screen. When GROUP mode is on, Titles applies to all worksheets in the file.

To freeze titles on-screen

1. If you want column headings at the top of the screen, move the cell pointer so that the column headings you want to freeze on-screen occupy the top rows of the spreadsheet.

   If you want row headings along the extreme left edge of the screen, move the cell pointer so that the columns containing the extreme left-row headings are at the left edge of the screen.

2. Move the cell pointer one row below the lowest row to be used as a title, and one column to the right of the column(s) to be used as title(s).

3. Type /WT.

4. Select Both, Horizontal, Vertical, or Clear.

/Worksheet Window

Purpose

Displays active worksheets and files from multiple viewpoints. Displays portions of three worksheets, two views of the same worksheet, part of a worksheet and a graph, or a maplike overview of the worksheet.

To display a worksheet window

1. Type /WW.

2. Select one of the following:

Menu Item	Function
Horizontal	Splits the worksheet into two horizontal windows at the cell pointer.
Vertical	Splits the worksheet into two vertical windows at the cell pointer.
Sync	Synchronizes two windows so that they scroll together.

Unsync	Enables you to scroll two windows independently of each other.
Clear	Reverts to one window.
Map	Switches between the worksheet and a map view of the worksheet. The map view displays labels as quote marks ("), and values as number signs (#), and plus signs (+) in formulas or annotated numbers. **E**nable turns on the map; **D**isable turns off the map.
Perspective	Stacks three worksheets so that portions of each are displayed.
Graph	Displays the graph in the worksheet area to the right of the cell pointer. Changing data changes the graph.
Display	Switches between two screen display modes you selected at installation. Choose **1** for the first mode you installed and **2** for the second mode.

WYSIWYG COMMAND REFERENCE

1-2-3 Releases 3.1 and 3.1+ provide you with the tools you need to present your spreadsheets in an attractive format. This section provides an alphabetical listing of all the Wysiwyg commands available when you press colon (:). Before you can use Wysiwyg commands, you must load the add-in into memory.

To load the add-in into memory

1. Press **Alt-F10** (Addin).

2. Type **L**.

3. Highlight WYSIWYG.PLC and press Enter.

4. If you do not want to assign a function key to Wysiwyg, press N. To assign a function key, press 1, 2, or 3. These numbers correspond to function keys Alt-F7, Alt-F8, and Alt-F9.

5. Press Q.

:Display Colors

Purpose

Specifies worksheet colors for background, text, cell pointer, grid, worksheet frame, drop shadows, negative values, and data in unprotected ranges. Also modifies the hue of the eight colors that 1-2-3 uses with Wysiwyg.

Reminder

:Display Colors is the only :Display command that affects the worksheets or graphics you print; it only affects worksheets and graphics if you have a color printer.

To display colors

1. Type :DC.

2. Select one of the following commands. All commands (except for Replace) prompt you to select a color from Black, White, Red, Green, Dark-Blue, Cyan, Yellow, and Magenta.

Menu Item	*Function*
Background	Determines the color of the worksheet background.
Text	Determines the color for worksheet text.
Unprot	Determines the color for data in ranges where global protection has

	been removed with the /Range Unprot command.
Cell-Pointer	Determines the color for the cell pointer.
Grid	Determines the color for the worksheet gridlines set with the :Display Options Grid Yes command.
Frame	Determines the color for the worksheet frame.
Neg	Determines the color of negative values.
Lines	Determines the color for lines added to the worksheet with the :Format Lines command.
Shadow	Determines the color for drop shadows added to the worksheet with the :Format Lines Shadow Set command.
Replace	Modifies the hue of the eight Wysiwyg colors. Select a number from 0 to 63.

Note

To update Wysiwyg so it uses the new color settings in future sessions, select :Display Default Update.

:Display Default

Purpose

Creates a new set of default display settings. Also replaces current display settings with default display settings.

Reminder

The default display settings are stored in the Wysiwyg configuration file WYSIWYG3.CNF. 1-2-3 uses this file automatically whenever you load Wysiwyg into memory.

To change the display default settings

Type **:DD**. Then select from these menu items:

Menu Item	Function
Restore	Replaces the current display settings with the default display settings.
Update	Saves the current display settings as the default display settings.

:Display Font-Directory

Purpose

Specifies the directory where 1-2-3 looks for the fonts that it needs for the screen display and for printing.

Reminder

If you select a directory without font files, 1-2-3 displays and prints in the system font, which is `Courier`.

To specify the font directory

Type **:DF**. Then press **Esc** to delete the current directory setting. Type the drive letter and path name of the new directory.

Notes

The default font directory is the WYSIWYG subdirectory of the 1-2-3 Release 3.1 or 3.1+ program directory; for example, C:\123R3\WYSIWYG>.

To update Wysiwyg so it uses the new font directory settings in future sessions, select **:D**isplay **D**efault **U**pdate.

:Display Mode

Purpose

Changes between graphics and text display modes, and between black-and-white and color.

Reminder

Graphics display mode is the Wysiwyg default mode. Color and black-and-white work only in graphics display mode.

To modify the display mode

Type **:DM**. Then select one of the following choices:

Menu Item	Function
Graphics	Sets the worksheet display to look like the final printed output.
Text	Sets the worksheet display to look like the standard 1-2-3 display, not Wysiwyg.
B&W	Sets worksheet display to black-and-white (monochrome).
Color	Sets worksheet display to color.

Notes

In graphics display mode, the screen display looks like your final printed output.

To update Wysiwyg so that it uses the new mode settings in future sessions, select **:D**isplay **D**efault **U**pdate.

:Display Options

Purpose

Affects the display of gridlines, page breaks, worksheet frame, and the cell pointer. Also affects brightness.

To modify the display options

Type **:DO**. Then select one of the following choices:

Menu Item	Function
Frame	Changes the appearance of or hides the 1-2-3 worksheet frame. Select from the following frame settings:
	1-2-3 displays the standard worksheet frame.
	Enhanced displays a worksheet frame with lines highlighting the frame, each row, and column.
	Relief displays a sculpted worksheet frame, replaces the cyan color with gray, and turns brightness to high.
	Special replaces the column letters and row numbers of the worksheet frame with horizontal and vertical rulers in the following way:
	Characters displays rulers in 10-point characters with 6 lines per inch; **I**nches displays rulers in inches; **M**etric displays rulers in centimeters; **P**oints/Picas displays rulers in points and picas; **N**one hides the worksheet frame.
Grid	**Y**es turns on the worksheet gridlines; **N**o turns them off.
Page-Breaks	**Y**es displays page break symbols; **N**o hides them.

Wysiwyg Command Reference

Cell-Pointer
: **S**olid displays the cell pointer as a solid-colored rectangle. **O**utline displays it as a rectangular border around the current cell or range.

Intensity
: **N**ormal shows the display at normal intensity. **H**igh shows the display at high intensity.

Notes

The default worksheet frame for Wysiwyg is **E**nhanced.

To insert page breaks, set a print range with **:P**rint **R**ange**S**et, and then use **:W**orksheet**P**age.

To update Wysiwyg so that it uses the new options settings in future sessions, select **:D**isplay **D**efault **U**pdate.

:Display Rows

Purpose

Specifies the number of rows that 1-2-3 displays on the screen while in graphics mode.

Reminder

1-2-3 may display fewer or more rows than you specify; the number depends on the size of the default font and your graphics adapter card.

To specify the number of rows to be displayed

Type **:DR**. Then type a number from **16** to **60** and press **Enter**.

Notes

1-2-3 can display from 16 to 60 rows. The default number depends on the display mode you selected during installation.

To update Wysiwyg so that it uses the new rows setting in future sessions, select :Display Default Update.

:Display Zoom

Purpose

Enlarges or reduces the worksheet cells and affects the number of rows and columns the screen can display.

To enlarge or reduce worksheet cells

Type :DZ. Then select one of the following commands:

Menu Item	Function
Tiny	Reduces cells to 63 percent of normal size.
Small	Reduces cells to 87 percent of normal size.
Normal	Displays cells at normal size (100 percent).
Large	Enlarges cells to 125 percent of normal size.
Huge	Enlarges cells to 150 percent of normal size.
Manual	Reduces or enlarges cells according to a scale factor from 25 to 400. Type a number from 25 to 400 and press Enter.

Note

To update Wysiwyg so that it uses the new zoom setting in future sessions, select :Display Default Update.

:Format Bold

Purpose

Changes data in a cell or range of cells from normal to bold or vice versa.

To boldface data

1. Type :FB.

2. Select one of the following commands:

Menu Item	Function
Set	Changes data in a cell or cell range to bold.
Clear	Changes data in a cell or cell range to normal.

3. Specify the cell or cell range.

:Format Color

Purpose

Displays and prints cell or cell ranges in seven colors.

Reminder

You need a color monitor to display colors and a color printer to print colors.

To select color text

1. Type :FC.

2. Select one of the following commands:

Menu Item	Function
Text	Changes the color of text in a cell or cell range. Colors can be Normal, Red, Green, Dark-Blue, Cyan, Yellow, and Magenta.

Menu Item	Function
Background	Changes the color of the background of a cell or cell range. Colors can be Normal, Red, Green, Dark-Blue, Cyan, Yellow, and Magenta.
Negative	Assigns a color for negative values in a range. Select Normal or Red.
Reverse	Switches the background and text colors in a cell or cell range.

3. Specify the cell or cell range.

Notes

Normal returns the color of the range to the color set with :Display Colors.

To display negative values in a color other than red, use :Display Colors Negative.

:Format Font

Purpose

Changes the font of a cell or cell range, specifies the default font for a file, replaces fonts in the current font set, updates and restores the default font set, and saves font libraries in files on disk.

Reminder

You can use up to eight fonts in any file.

To select fonts

Type :FF. Then select one of the following commands:

Menu Item	Function
1 to 8	Changes the font of a cell or cell range to the numbered font after you specify the range.

Replace
: Replaces one of the eight fonts in the current font set. **1** to **8** selects the font to replace. **S**wiss, **D**utch, **C**ourier, **X**Symbol, and **O**ther selects a typeface. Enter a number from **3** to **72** to select a point size.

Default
: **R**estore replaces the current font set with the default font set. **U**pdate creates a new default font set.

Library
: Determines factors regarding a font library file. **R**etrieve loads the font set you specify from those that you saved on disk previously. **S**ave stores the current font set in a font library file on disk under the name you specify. **E**rase deletes from disk the font library file you specify.

Notes

Fonts **1** to **8** comprise the current font set shown on the screen when you select **:**Format **F**ont.

1-2-3 automatically adds the extension AF3 to font libraries unless you enter a different extension.

:Format Italics

Purpose

Changes data in a cell or range of cells from standard to italics or vice versa.

To italicize data

1. Type **:FI**.
2. Select one of the following commands:

Menu Item	Function
Set	Changes data in a cell or cell range to italics.
Clear	Removes italics from data in a cell or cell range.

3. Specify the cell or cell range.

:Format Lines

Purpose

Draws single, double, or wide lines along the left, right, top, and bottom edges of cells or cell ranges, and adds a drop shadow to cells or cell ranges.

Reminder

Use **O**utline to draw lines around the edges of a cell or cell range. Use **A**ll to draw lines around the edges of all cells in a range.

To add lines to the worksheet

1. Type **:FL**.

2. Select one of the following commands:

Menu Item	Function
Outline	Draws a single line around the edges of a cell or cell range.
Left	Draws a single line along the left edge of a cell or cell range.
Right	Draws a single line along the right edge of a cell or cell range.
Top	Draws a single line along the top edge of a cell or cell range.

Bottom	Draws a single line along the bottom edge of a cell or cell range.
All	Draws a single line around the edges of all cells in a range.
Double	Draws a double line where you specify. Select from **O**utline, **L**eft, **R**ight, **T**op, **B**ottom, and **A**ll.
Wide	Draws a thick line where you specify. Select from **O**utline, **L**eft, **R**ight, **T**op, **B**ottom, and **A**ll.
Clear	Removes lines from a cell or cell range as you specify. Select from **O**utline, **L**eft, **R**ight, **T**op, **B**ottom, and **A**ll.
Shadow	**S**et adds a drop shadow to a cell or cell range. **C**lear removes a drop shadow.

3. Specify the cell or cell range.

:Format Reset

Purpose

Removes all formatting from a cell or cell range, and returns font and color settings to the defaults that were set with the **:D**isplay commands.

To remove Wysiwyg formatting

Type **:FR**. Then specify the cell or cell range.

Note

:Format **R**eset does not affect formats set with **/R**ange **F**ormat, **/W**orksheet **G**lobal **F**ormat, or the Wysiwyg formatting sequences.

:Format Shade

Purpose

Adds light, dark, or solid shading to a cell or cell range. Also removes shading from a cell or cell range.

Reminder

Solid shading hides the data in a cell or cell range unless you use :Format Color Text to select another color for the data.

To add shading

1. Type :FS.

2. Select one of the following commands:

Menu Item	Function
Light	Adds light shading to a cell range.
Dark	Adds dark shading to a cell range.
Solid	Adds solid shading to a cell range.
Clear	Removes shading from a cell range.

3. Specify the cell or cell range.

Note

Solid shading prints in black, even if you have a color printer.

:Format Underline

Purpose

Adds a single, double, or wide underline to a cell or cell range. Also removes underlining.

Reminder

Underlining appears only under data. It does not appear in blank cells or blank parts of a cell.

To add underlining

1. Type **:FU**.

2. Select one of the following commands:

Menu Item	Function
Single	Adds a single underline to a cell range.
Double	Adds a double underline to a cell range.
Wide	Adds a thick underline to a cell range.
Clear	Removes underlining from a cell range.

3. Specify the cell or cell range.

Notes

Underlining is the same color as that selected with the **:D**isplay **C**olors **T**ext command.

Use the **:F**ormat **L**ines command to underline blank cells.

:Graph Add

Purpose

Adds a graphic to a worksheet.

To add a graphic

Type **:GA**. Then select one of the following commands:

Menu Item	Function
Current	Adds the current graph to the worksheet when you specify the single-sheet range in which you want the graphic to appear.

Menu Item	Function
Named	Adds a named graph from the current file to the worksheet when you specify a named graph from the current file, and then specify the single-sheet range in which you want the graphic to appear.
PIC	Adds a 1-2-3 graph saved in a PIC file to the worksheet when you specify a graph file with a PIC extension, and then specify the single-sheet range in which you want the graph to appear.
Metafile	Adds a graphic saved in a CGM file to the worksheet when you specify a file with a CGM extension, and then specify the single-sheet range in which you want the graphic to appear.
Blank	Adds a blank graphic placeholder to the worksheet when you specify the single-sheet range in which you want the graphic to appear.

Notes

1-2-3 automatically sizes the graphic to fit in the specified range.

If you are designing a worksheet and know where you want to add a graphic but do not yet have the 1-2-3 graph or graphic metafile, use **:G**raph **A**dd **B**lank to add a blank placeholder the size of the graphic you will eventually add. Later, you can use **:G**raph **S**ettings **G**raph to replace the blank placeholder with the actual graphic.

:Graph Compute

Purpose

Updates all graphics in all active files.

To update graphs

Type **:GC**.

Note

1-2-3 updates current and named 1-2-3 graphs and blank placeholders with every worksheet recalculation unless you change the default by selecting **:G**raph **S**ettings **S**ync **N**o.

:Graph Edit

Purpose

Moves the graphics that you added to the worksheet with **:G**raph **A**dd to the graphics editing window. You can then edit and enhance a graphic with the **:G**raph **E**dit commands.

Reminders

You must be in graphics display mode to use the **:G**raph **E**dit commands.

You must select, or identify, objects and underlying graphics in the graphics editing window to edit, move, rearrange, or transform them with the **:G**raph **E**dit commands. You select objects with the **:G**raph **E**dit **S**elect commands or with the mouse.

To edit a graphic

1. Type **:GE**.

2. Specify the graphic to edit by either specifying a cell in the range that the graphic occupies or by pressing **F3** (Name) and selecting the graphic from the list 1-2-3 displays.

3. Select one of the following commands:

Menu Item	Function
Add	Adds objects such as text, geometric shapes, and freehand drawings to a graphic.
Select	Selects a single object, a group of objects, or a graphic to edit in the graphic editing window.
Edit	Changes the appearance of objects added to a graphic.
Color	Specifies colors for a graphic and objects added to it.
Transform	Changes the orientation or size of a graphic and objects added.
Rearrange	Copies, moves, deletes and restores, locks and unlocks, and determines the placement of objects added to a graphic.
View	Enlarges and reduces areas of the graphics editing window.
Options	In the graphics editing window, adds gridlines, changes the size of the cursor, or magnifies fonts.

4. Many of the above commands require moving a cursor that appears on the screen after a command is issued; use the pointer keys or mouse to move the cursor. Some commands require anchoring the cursor after moving it; use the **space bar** or left mouse button to anchor the cursor. Press **Enter** or double-click the left mouse button to complete an operation.

Notes

You can move a graphic to the graphics editing window any time 1-2-3 is in READY mode by double-clicking the graphic with the left mouse button.

Wysiwyg Command Reference

To add the contents of a cell in an active file to a graphic with :**G**raph **E**dit **A**dd **T**ext, type \ (backslash) followed by the name or address of the cell. Press **Enter**. If you enter a range name or address, Wysiwyg adds the contents of the first cell in the range.

You can position an object you want to add to a graphic by using x-coordinates and y-coordinates as anchor points. Instead of using the mouse or pointer keys to move the cursor to a location, type **x,y** where x is an x-coordinate from 0 to 4095 and y is a y-coordinate from 0 to 4095.

Then, if you are adding a line of text or anchoring the first point of a line, polygon, rectangle, ellipse, or freehand drawing, click the left mouse button or press the **space bar**. If you are completing a line, polygon, rectangle, ellipse or freehand drawing, double-click the left mouse button or press **Enter**.

:Graph Goto

Purpose

Moves the cell pointer to a specific graphic in the worksheet.

To move the cell pointer to a graphic

Type **:GG**. Then type the name of the graphic, point to the name of the graphic and press **Enter**, or type a cell address that lies within the range the graphic occupies.

:Graph Move

Purpose

Moves a graphic to another range in the worksheet.

To move a graphic

1. Type **:GM**.

2. Select the graphic to move by specifying a cell in the range that the graphic occupies or by pressing **F3** (Name) and selecting the graphic from the list that 1-2-3 displays.

3. Specify the first cell of the new range for the graphic.

Notes

:Graph **M**ove does not change the number of rows and columns in the range that the graphic occupies. If you move the graphic to a range with different row heights or column widths, however, 1-2-3 automatically resizes the graphic to fit in the new range.

:Graph **M**ove does not affect any data that may be underneath the graphic you move to another range.

:Graph Remove

Purpose

Deletes a graphic from the worksheet.

Reminder

:Graph **R**emove does not delete the actual named graph, graph file, graphic metafile, or current graph settings from memory or from disk. Also, it does not affect any data that may be underneath the graphic you delete from the worksheet.

To delete a graphic

1. Type **:GR**.

2. Select the graphic to remove by entering a cell address in the range that the graphic occupies or by pressing **F3** (Name) and selecting the graphic from the list that 1-2-3 displays.

3. Press **Enter**.

Notes

To specify more than one graphic to remove, specify a range that contains more than one graphic.

If you delete a graphic from the worksheet with :Graph Remove, you lose any enhancements you made to the graphic with the :Graph Edit commands.

:Graph Settings

Purpose

Moves and replaces graphics in the worksheet, turns on or off the display of graphics, makes graphics in the worksheet transparent or opaque, and makes 1-2-3 graphs in the worksheet update automatically when the data changes on which the graphs are based.

To specify graph settings

1. Type :GS.

2. Select one of the following commands:

Menu Item	Function
Graph	Replaces a graphic in the worksheet with another graphic. Once you specify the graphic to replace, you may select one of the following choices:

   Current replaces the specified graphic with the current graph.

   Named replaces the specified graphic with a named graph.

   PIC replaces the specified graphic with a 1-2-3 graph saved in a PIC file.

Menu Item	Function
	Metafile replaces the specified graphic with a graphic saved in a CGM file.
	Blank replaces the specified graphic with a blank placeholder.
Range	Resizes the range a graphic occupies or moves a graphic in the worksheet to a specified range.
Sync	Controls whether a graph is updated automatically to reflect changes in the data on which it is based. **Y**es makes a named or current graph in the worksheet update these changes automatically; **N**o turns off the feature.
Display	**Y**es displays a selected graphic in the worksheet; **N**o displays a selected graphic as shaded rectangles in the worksheet.
Opaque	**Y**es hides worksheet data underneath a selected graphic; **N**o makes worksheet data underneath a selected graphic visible.

3. Specify or select a graphic by specifying a cell in the range that the graphic occupies, or by pressing **F3** (Name) and selecting the graphic from the list that 1-2-3 displays. To specify more than one graphic, specify a range that contains more than one graphic.

4. Resize a graphic, if desired, by using the mouse or pointer keys to adjust the size of the range. Press **Enter**.

Notes

If you used **:G**raph **E**dit **C**olor **B**ackground to make the color of the range the graphic occupies transparent,

Wysiwyg Command Reference

1-2-3 does not display anything in the worksheet when you select **:G**raph **S**ettings **D**isplay **N**o.

:Graph **S**ettings **G**raph does not remove any enhancements made with the **:G**raph **E**dit commands. To replace a graphic and its enhancements, use **:G**raph **R**emove to remove the graphic and enhancements from the worksheet, then use **:G**raph **A**dd to add a different graphic.

:Graph View

Purpose

Temporarily removes the worksheet from the screen and displays a graphic saved in a PIC or CGM file on the full screen.

To display a graphic

1. Type **:GV**.

2. Select one of the following commands:

Menu Item	Function
PIC	Displays a list of 1-2-3 graphs saved in PIC files.
Metafile	Displays a list of graphics saved in CGM files.

3. Select the graphic to display and press **Enter**.

4. When you finish viewing the graphic, press any key to remove it and redisplay the worksheet.

:Graph Zoom

Purpose

Temporarily removes the worksheet from the screen and displays a specified graphic in the worksheet on the full screen.

To display a worksheet graphic on the full screen

1. Type **:GZ**.

2. Specify the graphic to display on the full screen by specifying a cell in the range the graphic occupies, or by pressing **F3** (Name) and selecting the graphic from the list 1-2-3 displays.

3. When you finish viewing the graphic, press any key to redisplay the worksheet.

:Named-Style

Purpose

Defines a named style or collection of Wysiwyg formats taken from a single cell, and then applies the named style to one or more ranges in the current file.

Reminder

Each file can contain up to eight named styles.

To define and apply a style

1. Type **:N**.

2. Select one of the following commands:

Menu Item	Function
1–8	Formats one or more ranges with the named styles defined with **:N**amed-Style **D**efine.
Define	Creates a named style for the Wysiwyg formats in a specified cell.

3. Specify the cell or cell range.

4. For **:N**amed-Style **D**efine, type a name of up to six characters and press **Enter**.

5. For **:N**amed-Style **D**efine, type a description of up to 37 characters and press **Enter**.

:Print Configuration

Purpose

Specifies the printer, printer interface, font cartridges, orientation, resolution, and paper-feed method.

Reminder

If you select Interface 8 or 9 (COM1 or COM2), you must use the operating system MODE command to set the baud rate and other communications settings for the serial port.

To specify print configuration options

Type :PC. Then select one of the following commands:

Menu Item	Function
Printer	Selects the printer on which to print a specified range when you select a number (1–9) or letter.
Interface	Specifies the interface, or port, that connects your computer to the printer when you select a number from 1–9. Also selects the baud rate for serial ports from a second-level set of numbers from 1–9 (the numbers correspond to baud rates from 110 to 19,200).
1st-Cart	Specifies a font cartridge or font card for your printer to use when you select a font-cartridge file or font-card file.

Note

If you redefine a named style, 1-2-3 automatically reformats any ranges formatted with that named style.

Menu Item	Function
2nd-Cart	Specifies a second font cartridge or font card for your printer to use when you select a second font-cartridge file or font-card file.
Orientation	Determines whether Wysiwyg prints in **P**ortrait mode or **L**andscape mode, provided Landscape mode is available on your printer.
Resolution	Specifies **F**inal (high) or **D**raft (low) resolution print mode.
Bin	Specifies the paper-feed option for your printer as follows:

Reset clears the current bin setting.

Single-Sheet selects a printer's single-sheet feeder.

Manual selects a printer's manual paper-feed option.

Upper-Tray selects a printer's top paper tray.

Lower-Tray selects a printer's bottom paper tray.

Note

To print on a network printer, select from Interface **5** (LPT1), **6** (LPT2), **7** (LPT3), **8** (COM1), or **9** (COM2).

:Print File

Purpose

Prints a range to an encoded file. The file can include 1-2-3 data, graphics, and printer codes for all Wysiwyg options, such as fonts, colors, line spacing, and print

Wysiwyg Command Reference

compression. The printer codes Wysiwyg uses are specific to your current printer.

Reminder

You cannot read an encoded file back into 1-2-3.

To print a range to an encoded file

1. Specify a print range with :**P**rint **R**ange.

2. Select the **F**ile option.

3. Name the encoded file and press **Enter**.

4. If you are updating an existing encoded file, select **C**ancel to return 1-2-3 to READY mode without saving an encoded file or select **R**eplace to write over the encoded file on disk with the current file.

Note

Wysiwyg automatically adds the extension ENC to encoded files unless you specify a different extension.

:Print Go

Purpose

Sends data to a printer.

To send data to a printer

Specify a print range with :**P**rint **R**ange **S**et. Then check that the printer is on-line and the paper is at the top of a page. Type **G**.

Notes

To stop printing and cancel other Wysiwyg and 1-2-3 print jobs that are waiting to print, use /**P**rint **C**ancel.

To temporarily stop printing, use /**P**rint **S**uspend; use /**P**rint **R**esume to continue printing.

:Print Info

Purpose

Removes or redisplays the Wysiwyg print status screen that overlays the worksheet when you select :Print.

Reminder

1-2-3 removes the Wysiwyg print status screen if it is displayed, or displays the screen if it is not displayed.

To remove or display the Wysiwyg print status screen

Type :PI.

Note

You can also press F6 (Window) to remove or display the Wysiwyg print status screen when you are using the :Print menu.

:Print Layout

Purpose

Controls the page layout, or the overall positioning and appearance of the page.

Reminder

1-2-3 saves page layout settings for a worksheet file in that file's corresponding format file.

To set the page layout

1. Type :PL.

2. Select one of the following commands:

Menu Item	Function
Page-Size	Specifies the length and width of the page when you select 1–7. Another option, Custom, permits you to enter a number for the page length and a number for the page width.

Wysiwyg Command Reference

Margins Sets Left, Right, Top, and Bottom margins when you enter a number followed by "in" or "mm" and press Enter.

Titles Creates page headers and footers with the Header and Footer commands, and clears them with the Clear Header, Clear Footer, or Clear Both commands.

Borders Specifies one or more rows to print at the top of every page and above every print range with the Top command; specifies one or more columns to print at the left of every page and print range with the Left command; and clears these borders with the Clear Top, Clear Left, or Clear All commands.

Compression Compresses or expands a print range as follows:

None removes compression or expansion from a print range.

Manual compresses the print range when you type a number from 15 to 99 and press Enter. It expands the print range when you type a number from 101 to 1000 and press Enter.

Automatic compresses a print range automatically, by up to a factor of seven, with the goal of fitting the range on one printed page whenever possible.

Default Sets the default page layout. Update creates a new default page layout setting; Restore replaces

Menu Item	Function
	the current page layout settings with the default page layout settings.
Library	Enables you to Retrieve, Save, or Erase page layout libraries on disk after you specify the name of the page layout library file.

3. If you select :PLPC, enter numbers in inches by typing the number followed by "in" and pressing Enter; enter numbers in millimeters by typing the number followed by "mm" and pressing Enter.

If you select :PLTH or :PLTF, type the header or footer at the prompt and press Enter.

If you select :PLBT, :PLBL, or :PLBC, specify a range that includes the rows or columns you want to use as a border.

If you select :PLLS to update an existing layout library, select Cancel to return 1-2-3 to READY mode without saving the current layout library or select Replace to write over the layout library on disk with the current layout library.

Notes

Type cm to denote a setting in centimeters; Wysiwyg converts the setting to millimeters automatically.

Do not include in your print range the rows and columns you specified as borders, or Wysiwyg prints those rows and columns twice.

Wysiwyg prints headers on the line below the top margin and footers on the line above the bottom margin. Wysiwyg always leaves two blank lines, measured in the default font, between printed data and the header or footer.

Wysiwyg uses four symbols to format headers and footers: # (pound sign) for page numbers, @ (at sign) for the current date, | (vertical bar) for alignment, and \ (backslash) to copy cell contents.

:Print Preview

Purpose

Temporarily removes the worksheet from the screen and displays the print range as Wysiwyg will format it for printing, page by page.

To display the print range as it will appear printed

Type **:PP**. Then press any key except Esc to cycle through the pages, or press **Esc** to redisplay the worksheet.

:Print Range

Purpose

Specifies or cancels the print range, which is the data Wysiwyg prints when you select **:P**rint **G**o or **:P**rint **F**ile.

Reminder

The print range can include any number of ranges in the current file.

To specify or cancel the print range

1. Type **:PR**.

2. Select **S**et to specify the print range; select **C**lear to clear the settings for the current print range.

3. If you select **S**et, specify the print range to set and press **Enter**.

Notes

If the print range includes a long label, include in the print range the cells that the long label overlaps as well as the cell in which you entered the long label.

To set multiple ranges as the print range, place an argument separator, such as a comma or semicolon, after each range to separate it from the next range.

In graphics display mode, the boundaries of the print range appear as dashed lines along the edges of the print range. The dashed lines remain on the screen until you clear the print range with **:P**rint **R**ange **C**lear.

:Print Settings

Purpose

Specifies which pages of a print range to print, the number of copies to print, whether to print the worksheet frame and gridlines, and whether to pause for manual paper feed. The **:P**rint **S**ettings command also controls page numbering.

Reminder

The Wysiwyg print settings are separate from the 1-2-3 print settings and, except for the **F**rame and **G**rid settings, affect only the current Wysiwyg session.

To specify print settings

1. Type **:PS**.

2. Select one of the following commands:

Menu Item	*Function*
Begin	Specifies the number of the page at which to begin printing.
End	Specifies the last page to print.
Start-Number	Specifies the page number of the first page in the print range.
Copies	Specifies the number of copies to print.
Wait	Specifies if the printing pauses after each page. **N**o does not pause printing after each page; **Y**es pauses printing after each page.

Wysiwyg Command Reference

Grid — Specifies if the worksheet gridlines are printed with the print range. **N**o does not print worksheet gridlines; **Y**es prints worksheet gridlines.

Frame — Specifies if the worksheet frame is printed with the print range. **N**o does not print the worksheet frame; **Y**es prints the worksheet frame.

Reset — Returns the Wysiwyg print settings to the defaults.

3. If you select **B**egin, **E**nd, **S**tart-Number, or **C**opies, type the appropriate number and press **Enter**.

    If you select **W**ait **Y**es, Wysiwyg prompts you to insert the next sheet of paper after it prints each page. Insert the next sheet of paper and then select **/P**rint **R**esume.

Notes

The beginning and ending page numbers depend on the page numbering you specify with **:P**rint **S**ettings **S**tart-Number.

Wysiwyg prints the standard 1-2-3 worksheet frame regardless of how you choose to display the worksheet frame with **:D**isplay **O**ptions **F**rame.

:Quit

Purpose
Returns 1-2-3 to READY mode.

To return to READY mode
Type **:Q**.

:Special Copy

Purpose

Copies all Wysiwyg formats in one range of an active file to another range of an active file. You can make one or more copies.

Reminder

:Special Copy does not copy data, graphics in the worksheet, or 1-2-3 formats you set with the /Range Format or /Worksheet Global Format commands.

To copy Wysiwyg formats

1. Type :SC.

2. Specify the range from which you want to copy formats and press Enter.

3. Specify the range to which you want to copy formats and press Enter.

:Special Export

Purpose

Creates a file with the font set, formats, named styles, and graphics in a Wysiwyg format file (FM3).

To export to a Wysiwyg format file

1. Type :SE.

2. Specify a format file to which to export and press Enter.

3. If you are updating an existing format file, select Cancel to return 1-2-3 to READY mode without exporting the current format file; select Replace to write over the format file on disk with a copy of the current format file.

Notes

1-2-3 automatically exports to a Wysiwyg format file (FM3) unless you enter a different extension. To export to an Impress format file, enter the extension FMT; to export to an Allways format file, enter the extension ALL.

If the file from which you export contains current or named graphs, 1-2-3 exports only their positions in the worksheet and enhancements made with the :Graph Edit commands, not the graphs themselves.

Many Wysiwyg features are not available in Allways and are therefore lost when you try to save them in an Allways format file (ALL).

:Special Import

Purpose

Applies the formats, named styles, font set, and graphics from a Wysiwyg format file (FM3), Impress format file (FMT), or Allways format file (ALL) on disk to the current file.

Reminder

1-2-3 automatically imports from a Wysiwyg format file (FM3) unless you enter a different extension. To import from an Impress format file, enter the extension FMT; to import from an Allways format file, enter the extension ALL.

To import from a Wysiwyg format file

1. Type :SI.

2. Select one of the following commands:

Menu Item	Function
All	Replaces all formats, named styles, and graphics in the current file with the formats, named styles, and graphics from a format file on disk.
Named-Styles	Replaces the named styles in the current file with the named styles from a Wysiwyg or Impress format file on disk.

Menu Item	Function
Fonts	Replaces the font set in the current file with the font set from a format file on disk.
Graphs	Copies graphics, including their positions in the worksheet and all enhancements added with the **:G**raph **E**dit commands, from a format file on disk to the current file.

3. Specify a format file from which to import and press **Enter**.

Notes

:Special **I**mport **G**raphs does not delete any graphic you already added to the current file with **:G**raph **A**dd.

If you import current or named graphs, 1-2-3 imports only their positions in the worksheet and enhancements made with the **:G**raph **E**dit commands, not the graphs themselves.

:Special Move

Purpose

Transfers the format of one range to another range in an active file and causes the cells that originally contained the formats to revert to the default formats. This command does not move data, graphics, or 1-2-3 formats set with the **/R**ange **F**ormat or **/W**orksheet **G**lobal **F**ormat commands.

To move a format

1. Type **:SM**.

2. Specify the range from which you want to move formats and press **Enter**.

3. Specify the range to which you want to move formats and press **Enter**.

Note

> The formats of the range from which you moved return to the defaults.

:Text Align

Purpose

> Changes the alignment of labels within a text range by changing their label prefixes.

To change the alignment of labels

1. Type **:TA**.

2. Select one of the following:

Menu Item	Function
Left	Aligns labels with the left edge of the text range.
Right	Aligns labels with the right edge of the text range.
Center	Centers labels in the text range.
Even	Aligns labels with both the left and right edges of the text range.

3. Specify the range within which you want to align labels. Press **Enter**.

Note

> If the file is in GROUP mode, **:T**ext **A**lign affects the corresponding range in all worksheets in the file.

:Text Clear

Purpose

> Clears the settings for a text range, but does not erase the data contained in the range or change any formatting

performed on the data using the :Text Reformat or :Text Edit commands.

To clear the settings for a text range

Type :TC. Then specify the text range whose settings you want to clear and press Enter.

Notes

If the file is in GROUP mode, :Text Clear affects the corresponding range in all worksheets in the file.

After you use :Text Clear, the formatting description {Text} no longer appears in the Control panel when the cell pointer is in the range.

:Text Edit

Purpose

Enables you to enter and edit labels in a text range directly in the worksheet.

To enter and edit labels in a specified range

1. Type :TE.

2. Specify the range in which you want to edit text and press Enter.

3. When you finish editing, press Esc to return 1-2-3 to READY mode.

Notes

When you issue the :Text Edit command, a cursor appears at the first character in the range and the mode indicator changes to LABEL.

:Text Edit permits you to enter text only in the range you specify. It does not place text in rows that are not included in the specified range.

You can press F3 when using :Text Edit to see a menu of formatting options you can apply to the text you enter or edit.

:Text Reformat

Purpose

Rearranges (justifies) a column of labels so that the labels fit within a text range.

Reminders

To use :Text Reformat, you must turn off global protection for the worksheet that contains the column of labels.

Using :Text Reformat on cells whose contents are used in formulas may change or invalidate the results of the formulas.

To justify a column of labels

1. Move the cell pointer to the first cell in the column of labels you want to rearrange.

2. Type :TR.

3. Specify the text range in which you want to rearrange labels and press Enter.

Notes

If the file is in GROUP mode, :Text Reformat affects the corresponding range in all worksheets in the file.

:Text Reformat affects labels in only the first column of a text range.

When Wysiwyg rearranges the text, it aligns all of the labels within the range depending on the first label's label prefix.

:Text Set

Purpose

Specifies a text range so you can use the :Text commands with labels in the range.

To specify a text range

Type **:TS**. Then specify the range you want to make a text range and press **Enter**.

Notes

If the file is in GROUP mode, **:T**ext **S**et affects the corresponding range in all worksheets in the file.

After you use **:T**ext **S**et, the formatting description {Text} appears in the Control panel when the cell pointer is in the range.

:Worksheet Column

Purpose

Sets the width of one or more columns and resets columns to the 1-2-3 global column width.

Reminder

The column widths you specify remain in effect even after you remove Wysiwyg from memory.

To set the width of one or more columns

1. Type **:WC**.

2. Select **S**et-Width to set the column width for one or more columns; select **R**eset-Width to reset one or more columns to the global column width.

3. If you selected **S**et-Width, specify the range of columns whose widths you want to set. Specify the new width either by typing a number from **1** to **20** and pressing **Enter**, or by using ← or → and pressing **Enter**.

   If you selected **R**eset-Width, specify the range of columns whose widths you want to reset to the global column width and press **Enter**.

Notes

If the file is in GROUP mode, **:W**orksheet **C**olumn affects the corresponding column in all worksheets in the file.

When the screen is split into two horizontal or vertical windows, the :Worksheet Column commands affect only the window in which the cell pointer is located. When you clear the windows, 1-2-3 uses the top or left window's column settings.

If you set the display of your worksheet frame with :Display Options Frame [Enhanced, Relief], you can use the mouse to set the width of a column whenever 1-2-3 is in READY mode. You can also use the mouse to hide or redisplay a column whenever 1-2-3 is in READY mode.

:Worksheet Page

Purpose

Inserts or removes horizontal or vertical page breaks that tell 1-2-3 to begin a new page when printing with the Wysiwyg :Print commands.

To insert or remove page breaks

Position the cell pointer in the leftmost column or top row on which you want a new page to start. Then type :WP. Select one of the following commands:

Menu Item	Function
Row	Inserts a horizontal page break.
Column	Inserts a vertical page break.
Delete	Removes vertical and/or horizontal page breaks from the current column and/or row.

Notes

If the file is in GROUP mode, 1-2-3 inserts page breaks in the corresponding location in all worksheets in the file when you select :Worksheet Page Column or :Worksheet Page Row. It also deletes page breaks in the corresponding location in all worksheets in the file when you select :Worksheet Page Delete.

1-2-3 inserts a dashed line along the left of the column for a vertical page break or along the top of the row for a horizontal page break. When you print data, 1-2-3 starts a new page at the row or column you specified.

To hide the dashed lines that symbolize page breaks on your screen, use :Display Options Page-Breaks No.

:Worksheet Row

Purpose

Sets the height of one or more rows. You can specify a height in points, or make 1-2-3 automatically set row heights to accommodate the largest font in a row.

To specify row height

1. Type :WR.

2. Select Set-Height to set the row height for one or more rows; select Auto to automatically set the height of one or more rows based on the size of the largest font in the row.

3. If you select Set-Height, specify the range of rows whose heights you want to set. You can then specify the row height, either by typing a number from 1 to 255 and pressing Enter, or by using ↑ and ↓ and pressing Enter.

   If you select Auto, specify the range of rows whose heights you want 1-2-3 to set automatically and press Enter.

Notes

If the file is in GROUP mode, then :Worksheet Row affects the corresponding row in all worksheets in the file. When the screen is split into two windows, :Worksheet Row affects both windows.

If you set the display of your worksheet frame with :Display Options Frame [Enhanced, Relief], you can use the mouse to set the height of a row whenever 1-2-3 is in READY mode. You can also use the mouse to hide or redisplay a row whenever 1-2-3 is in READY mode.

1-2-3 RELEASE 3.1+ ENHANCEMENT ADD-INS

The four enhancement add-ins for Release 3.1+, Auditor, Backsolver, Solver, and Viewer, are attached to 1-2-3 in the Add-In (Alt–F10) menu. To select and attach an add-in, follow these steps:

1. Activate the Add-In menu by pressing Alt–F10.
2. Select Load.
3. Highlight the add-in and press Enter.
4. Select a key to invoke the add-in. If you want to use Alt–F7, choose 1. Choose 2 for Alt–F8, 3 for Alt–F9, or No-Key if you don't want to invoke the add-in using function keys.
5. Select Quit to return to READY mode.

The Auditor Add-In

Purpose

Helps analyze worksheets to ensure accuracy. Shows how formula and data cells are dependent.

Reminder

You must attach the Auditor add-in and then invoke it (using the function key assigned) before using Auditor commands.

Circs

Purpose

Finds and identifies circular references.

Reminder

> 1-2-3 displays the CIRC indicator when a circular reference exists in the worksheet.

To find circular references

> Invoke Auditor and type **C**. Then specify the range for the list of cells. If more than one circular reference exists, select one of the listed cells.

Dependents

Purpose

> Identifies all cells that depend on the value of a specified cell.

To identify dependent cells

> 1. Invoke Auditor and type **D**.
> 2. Specify the source cell.
> 3. If you selected **O**ptions **L**ist, specify the output range for the dependents list. If you selected **O**ptions **T**race, select **F**orward, **B**ackward, or **Q**uit.

Formulas

Purpose

> Identifies all formulas in the audit range.

To identify formulas

> Invoke Auditor and type **F**. If you selected **O**ptions **L**ist, specify the output range for the dependents list. If you selected **O**ptions **T**race, select **F**orward, **B**ackward, or **Q**uit.

Options

Purpose

> Enables you to specify Auditor's settings.

To specify Auditor's settings

Invoke Auditor and type **O**. Then select the setting you want to change:

Menu Item	Function
Audit-Range	Specifies the area to be audited.
Highlight	Highlights all matching cells.
List	Generates a list of matching cells.
Quit	Returns to Auditor main menu.
Reset	**H**ighlight removes highlights previously added by Auditor.
	Options returns options to default settings.
Trace	Moves cell pointer to matching cells.

Precedents

Purpose

Identifies cells on which a specified cell depends.

To identify cells on which a specified cell depends

1. Invoke Auditor and type **P**.

2. Specify the dependent cell.

3. If you selected **O**ptions **L**ist, specify the output range for the precedents list. If you selected **O**ptions **T**race, select **F**orward, **B**ackward, or **Q**uit.

Recalc-List

Purpose

Identifies the order in which formulas are recalculated.

To identify the recalculation order

Invoke Auditor and type **R**. If you selected **O**ptions **L**ist, specify the output range for the precedents list. If you selected **O**ptions **T**race, select **F**orward, **B**ackward, or **Q**uit.

The Backsolver Add-In

Purpose

Changes the value of a single variable to produce a desired end result.

Reminder

You must attach the Backsolver add-in and then invoke it (using the function key assigned) before using Backsolver commands.

Adjustable

Purpose

Specifies the value to be changed.

Reminder

Backsolver changes a single cell. To solve problems with multiple adjustable cells, use the Solver add-in.

To specify the adjustable cell

Invoke Backsolver and type **A**. Then specify the adjustable cell.

Formula-Cell

Purpose

Specifies the formula that should equal a specified value.

To specify the formula that should equal a specified value

Invoke Backsolver and type **F**. Then specify the formula cell.

Solve

Purpose

Executes Backsolver.

To execute Backsolver

Invoke Backsolver and type **S**.

Value

Purpose

Specifies the value the formula should equal.

To specify the value the formula should equal

Invoke Backsolver and type **V**. Then specify the value or formula that evaluates to a value the formula cell should attain.

The Solver Add-In

Purpose

Provides optimal solutions to a series of equations with multiple variables. You specify values that are adjustable, constraints that must be met, and a value that should be either minimized or maximized.

Reminder

You must attach the Solver add-in and then invoke it (using the function key assigned) before using Solver commands.

Answer

Purpose

Displays the answers Solver found while examining the problem.

To display Solver answers

Invoke Solver and type **A**. Then select the answer you want to display:

Menu Item	Function
First	Displays the first answer found by Solver.
Last	Displays the last answer found by Solver.
Next	Displays the answer found by Solver following the currently displayed answer.
Optimal	Displays the optimal answer found by Solver.
Previous	Displays the answer found by Solver preceding the currently displayed answer.
Quit	Returns to the Solver main menu.
Reset	Returns the adjustable cells to their original values.

Define

Purpose

Specifies the conditions Solver should use to analyze the problem.

To specify the Solver conditions

Invoke Solver and type **D**. Then select the cells you want to define:

1-2-3 Release 3.1+ Enhancement Add-ins

Menu Item	Function
Adjustable	Defines the cells that should be adjusted to solve the problem.
Constraints	Specifies the formula cells that provide limits to the problem.
Optimal	Specifies the formula cell to be optimized.
	N-Minimize specifies that the value of the optimal cell should attain the smallest possible value.
	Reset specifies the problem should not use an optimal cell.
	X-Maximize specifies that the value of the optimal cell should attain the highest possible value.
Quit	Returns to the Solver main menu.

Options

Purpose
Defines the number of solutions Solver should attempt to find.

To define the number of Solver solutions
Invoke Solver and type **O**. Then specify the number of solutions (from **1** to **999**) that Solver should attempt to provide.

Report

Purpose
Determines which of seven reports Solver will display.

To determine which report Solver will display
Invoke Solver and type **R**. Then select the report you want to display:

Menu Item	Function
Answer	Displays the answers found by Solver.
Cells	Reports on the cells used in finding the solution.
Differences	Displays cells that vary by a specified amount in two different answers.
How	Explains the current answer.
Inconsistent	Reports on constraints that could not be met.
Quit	Returns to Solver main menu.
Unused	Reports on constraints that had no effect on the outcome.
What-If	Reports on latitude available in currently defined constraints.

The **C**ells, **D**ifferences, **I**nconsistent, **U**nused, and **W**hat-If selections contain the following subselections:

Menu Item	Function
Cell	Displays report information cell-by-cell in a report window.
	Next displays the next cell report window.
	Quit returns to the **R**eport menu.
Table	Displays report information in a new worksheet file following all open files.

Solve

Purpose

Directs Solver to attempt to find solutions to the problem.

1-2-3 Release 3.1+ Enhancement Add-ins

Reminder

Use **D**efine to specify at least the adjustable and constraint cells before selecting **S**olve.

To find solutions

Invoke Solver and type **S**. Then select the action you want Solver to perform:

Menu Item	Function
Continue	Directs Solver to attempt to find additional answers.
Guesses	Enables you to enter new values for adjustable cells.
	Guess specifies a new value for the currently displayed adjustable cell.
	Next displays the next adjustable cell.
	Quit returns to the **G**uesses menu.
	Solve directs Solver to again attempt to find answers.
Problem	Directs Solver to attempt to find answers (up to the number defined) using **O**ptions **N**umber-**A**nswers.

The Viewer Add-In

Purpose

Enables you to examine files before retrieving or opening them. Greatly simplifies creation of file linking formulas.

Reminder

You must attach the Viewer add-in and then invoke it (using the function key assigned) before using Viewer commands.

Browse

Purpose

Enables you to view the contents of text files. Can be helpful before issuing a /File Import Text command to ensure the correct text file is being imported.

To view the contents of text files

Invoke Viewer and type B. Then select the file you want to browse.

Link

Purpose

Displays worksheet files and creates formulas in the current worksheet linking it to the displayed file.

To link the current worksheet to another file

1. Invoke Viewer and type L.

2. Select the file you want to link into the current worksheet.

3. Press Enter to switch to the View window.

4. Highlight the cells to be linked and press Enter.

5. If the target cells contain data, select Yes to add the linking formulas or No to cancel the command.

Open

Purpose

Displays and opens additional worksheet files.

To display and open files

1. Invoke Viewer and type O.

2. Select After to open the new file after the current one, or Before to open it before the current file.

3. Select the file you want to open and press Enter. If necessary, enter the file password.

Retrieve

Purpose

Displays and retrieves a worksheet file (replacing the current file).

To display and retrieve a worksheet file

1. Invoke Viewer and type **R**.

2. If the current file has been modified, select **N**o to return to the worksheet or **Y**es to replace the current worksheet without saving it.

3. Select the file you want to open and press **Enter**. If necessary, enter the file password.

1-2-3 FUNCTIONS

This section provides all 1-2-3 functions in alphabetical order.

For an in-depth discussion of 1-2-3 functions, see Que's *Using 1-2-3 for DOS Release 3.1+,* Special Edition.

@@*(cell_address)*

@ABS*(x)*

@ACOS*(x)*

@ASIN*(x)*

@ATAN*(x)*

@ATAN2*(x,y)*

@AVG*(range)*

@CELL*(attribute,range)*

@CELLPOINTER*(attribute)*

@CHAR*(n)*

@CHOOSE*(offset,list)*

@CLEAN*(string)*

@CODE*(string)*

@COLS(*range*)

@COORD(*worksheet,column,row,absolute*)

@COS(*x*)

@COUNT(*range*)

@CTERM(*inf,fv,pv*)

@D360(*date1,date2*)

@DATE(*y,m,d*)

@DATEVALUE(*date_string*)

@DAVG(*input_range,field,criterion_range*)

@DAY(*date*)

@DCOUNT(*input_range,field,criterion_range*)

@DDB(*cost,salvage,life,period*)

@DGET(*input_range,field,criterion_range*)

@DMAX(*input_range,field,criterion_range*)

@DMIN(*input_range,field,criterion_range*)

@DQUERY(*external_function,arguments*)

@DSTD(*input_range,field,criterion_range*)

@DSTDS(*input_range,field,criterion_range*)

@DSUM(*input_range,field,criterion_range*)

@DVAR(*input_range,field,criterion_range*)

@DVARS(*input_range,field,criterion_range*)

@ERR

@EXACT(*string1,string2*)

@EXP(*x*)

@FALSE

@FIND(*search_string,string,start_number*)

@FV(*pmt,int,term*)

@HLOOKUP(*key,range,row_offset*)

@HOUR(*time*)

1-2-3 Functions

@IF*(test,true,false)*

@INDEX*(range,column,row,[worksheet])*

@INFO*(attribute)*

@INT*(x)*

@IRR*(guess,cashflows)*

@ISERR*(x)*

@ISNA*(x)*

@ISNUMBER*(x)*

@ISRANGE*(x)*

@ISSTRING*(x)*

@LEFT*(string,n)*

@LENGTH*(string)*

@LN*(x)*

@LOG*(x)*

@LOWER*(string)*

@MAX*(range)*

@MID*(string,start_number,n)*

@MIN*(range)*

@MINUTE*(time)*

@MOD*(x,y)*

@MONTH*(date)*

@N*(range)*

@NA

@NOW

@NPV*(int,cashflows)*

@PI

@PMT*(principal,int,term)*

@PROPER*(string)*

@PV*(pmt,int,term)*

@RAND

@RATE*(fv,pc,term)*

@REPEAT*(string,n)*

@REPLACE*(original_string,start_number,length, replacement_string)*

@RIGHT*(string,n)*

@ROUND*(x,precision)*

@ROWS*(range)*

@S*(range)*

@SECOND*(time)*

@SHEETS*(range)*

@SIN*(x)*

@SLN*(cost,salvage,life)*

@SQRT*(x)*

@STD*(range)*

@STDS*(range)*

@STRING*(numeric_value,decimal_places)*

@SUM*(range)*

@SUMPRODUCT*(range1,range2)*

@SYD*(cost,salvage,life,period)*

@TAN*(x)*

@TERM*(pmt,int,fv)*

@TIME*(hr,min,sec)*

@TIMEVALUE*(time_string)*

@TODAY

@TRIM*(string)*

@TRUE

@UPPER*(string)*

@VALUE*(string)*

@VAR*(range)*

@VARS(range)

@VDB(cost,salvage,life,start,end,[depreciation],[switch])

@VLOOKUP(key,change,column_offset)

@YEAR(date)

MACRO KEY NAMES

The keystroke instructions automate single-key activities (for example, Home, End, or Esc) within macros. Using {HOME} in a macro, for example, moves the cell pointer to the upper left corner of the active window.

Use the following macro instructions to perform certain key functions.

Instruction	Keyboard Key
~	Enter
{ABS}	F4 (Abs)
{ADDIN}	Alt-F10 (Addin)
{APP1}	Alt-F7 (App1)
{APP2}	Alt-F8 (App2)
{APP3}	Alt-F9 (App3)
{BS}	Backspace [←]
{BIGLEFT}	Shift-Tab
{BIGRIGHT}	Tab
{CALC}	F9 (Calc)
{CE}	Esc (to clear an entry; may be used more than once)
{DEL}	Del
{DOWN} or {D}	Down-arrow key [↓]
{EDIT}	F2 (Edit)

Instruction	Keyboard Key
{END}	End
{ESC}	Esc
{FILE}	Ctrl-End
{FIRSTCELL} or {FC}	Ctrl-Home
{FIRSTFILE} or {FF} or {FILE}{HOME}	Ctrl-End+Home
{GOTO}	F5 (GoTo)
{GRAPH}	F10 (Graph)
{HELP}	F1 (Help)
{HOME}	Home
{LASTCELL} or {LC}	End+Ctrl-Home
{LASTFILE} or {LF} or {FILE}{END}	Ctrl-End+Home
{LEFT} or {L}	Left-arrow key [←]
{MENU} or /	(Initiates the command menu)
{NAME}	F3 (Name)
{NEXTFILE} or {NF} or {FILE}{NS}	Ctrl-End+Ctrl-PgUp
{NEXTSHEET} or {NS}	Ctrl-PgUp
{PGDN}	PgDn
{PGUP}	PgUp

{PREVFILE} or {PF} or {FILE}{PS}	**Ctrl-End+Ctrl-PgDn**
{PREVSHEET} or {PS}	**Ctrl-PgDn**
{RIGHT} or {R}	**Right-arrow key** [→]
{QUERY}	**F7** (Query)
{TABLE}	**F8** (Table)
{UP} or {U}	**Up-arrow key** [↑]
{WINDOW}	**F6** (Window)
{ZOOM}	**Alt-F6** (Zoom)
{~}	Tilde (for Enter)
{{}	Open brace
{}}	Close brace

Note

Use the instruction {LEFT 3} to move the cell pointer three cells to the left.

ADVANCED MACRO COMMANDS

{?}

{APPENDBELOW *destination, source*}

{APPENDRIGHT *destination, source*}

{BEEP *number*} or {BEEP}

{BLANK *location*}

{BRANCH *location*}

{BREAKOFF}

{BREAKON}

{CLOSE}

{CONTENTS *destination,source,width,format*}

{DEFINE *loc1:Type1,...*}

{DISPATCH *location*}

{FILESIZE *location*}

{FOR *counter,start,stop,step,routine*}

{FORBREAK}

{FORM *input,call-table,include-keys,exclude-keys*}

{FRAMEOFF}

{FRAMEON}

{GET *location*}

{GETLABEL *prompt,location*}

{GETNUMBER *prompt,location*}

{GETPOS *location*}

{GRAPHOFF}

{GRAPHON *named-graph,*[*nodisplay*]}

{IF *condition*}

{INDICATE *string*}

{LET *location,expression*}

{LOOK *location*}

{MENUBRANCH *location*}

{MENUCALL *location*}

{ONERROR *branch,message*}

{OPEN *filename,access-mode*}

{PANELOFF}

{PANELON}

{PUT *range,col,row,value*}

{QUIT}

Advanced Macro Commands

{READ *bytecount,location*}
{READLN *location*}
{RECALC *location,condition,iterations*}
{RECALCCOL *location,condition,iterations*}
{RESTART}
{RETURN}
{SETPOS *file-position*}
{SYSTEM *command*}
{WAIT *argument*}
{WINDOWSOFF}
{WINDOWSON}
{WRITE *string*}
{WRITELN *string*}

1-2-3 for DOS Release 3.1+ Quick Reference

Index

Symbols

. (period) 1-2-3 key, 5
/ (slash) 1-2-3 key, 5
< (less-than sign) 1-2-3 key, 5
← key, 2
→ key, 2
↑ key, 2
↓ key, 2
1-2-3
  @functions, 133-137
  exiting, 59
    temporarily, 69
  keys, 5-6
  returning to READY
    mode, 113
  synchronizing with printer, 48

A

Abs (F4) function key, 4
active files, erasing from
  memory, 71
add-ins, loading into
  memory, 81
Addin (Alt-F10) function key, 5
Adjustable Backsolver
  add-in, 126
advanced macro commands,
  139-141
aligning text labels, 64
Answer Solver add-in, 128
App1 (Atl-F7) function key, 5
App2 (Alt-F8) function key, 5
App3 (Alt-F9) function key, 5
applying styles, 104
Auditor add-in, 123-125

B

Backsolver add-in, 126
Backspace 1-2-3 key, 5
blank files, 33
boldface, 89
Break 1-2-3 key, 5
Browse Viewer add-in, 132

C

Calc (F9) function key, 4
cell pointers
  moving
    to graphics, 99
    with mouse, 7
  restricting movement to
    unprotected cells, 63
cell-protection attributes, copying,
  13
cells
  assigning names, 64-66
  editing contents, 12
  enlarging/reducing in
    worksheets, 88
  identifying
    cells on which specified cell
      depends, 125
    dependent, 124
  restricting cell pointer to
    unprotected cells, 63
  selecting print format, 57
  shading, 94
  specifying adjustable, 126
  underlining, 94
Circs Auditor add-in, 123
circular references, finding, 123
clearing
  print settings, 49
  text range settings, 117
colors
  displaying, 82-83
  selecting color text, 89
columns
  adjusting width, 70
  deleting, 70
  inserting, 78
  inverting, 19
  printing on every page, 54
  setting width, 71, 120-121
command line, 1
Compose (Alt-F1) function
  key, 5
/Copy 1-2-3 command, 13

copying
  cell-protection attributes, 13
  formats, 13
  formulas, 13
  labels, 13
  records, 24
  to output range of worksheet
    records, 21
  values, 13
  Wysiwyg format, 114
Ctrl-← key, 2
Ctrl-→ key, 2
Ctrl-End+Ctrl-PgDn key
  combination, 4
Ctrl-End+Ctrl-PgUp key
  combination, 3
Ctrl-End+End key combination, 4
Ctrl-End+Home key
  combination, 4
Ctrl-Home key combination, 3
Ctrl-PgDn key combination, 3
Ctrl-PgUp key combination, 3

D

data
  italicizing, 91
  making boldface, 89
  moving, 46
  sending to printers, 107
  sorting, 25
  transposing, 68
/Data Distribution 1-2-3
  command, 14
/Data External Create 1-2-3
  command, 15
/Data External Delete/Reset
  1-2-3 command, 15
/Data External List 1-2-3
  command, 16
/Data External Other 1-2-3
  command, 16-18
/Data External Use 1-2-3
  command, 18
/Data Fill 1-2-3 command, 18
/Data Matrix 1-2-3 command, 19
/Data Parse 1-2-3 command, 19
/Data Query Criteria 1-2-3
  command, 20
/Data Query Delete 1-2-3
  command, 21
/Data Query Extract/Unique
  1-2-3 command, 21

/Data Query Find 1-2-3 command,
  22
/Data Query Input command, 23
/Data Query Modify 1-2-3
  command, 23
/Data Query Output 1-2-3
  command, 24
/Data Regression 1-2-3
  command, 25
/Data Sort 1-2-3 command, 25
/Data Table 1/2/3 1-2-3
  command, 26
/Data Table Labeled 1-2-3
  command, 27
data trends, 25
databases
  creating data frequency
    distribution for, 14
  external, 15-18
  searching for records in, 22
default
  display settings, changing, 84
  numeric format, defining, 74
Define Solver add-in, 128
defining styles, 104
deleting
  columns, 70
  files, 70
  graphics from worksheets, 100
  records from ranges, 21
  rows, 70
  tables from external
    databases, 15
  worksheets, 70
Dependents Auditor add-in, 124
directories
  changing, 31
  font, 84
disk drive, changing, 31
disks, erasing files from, 31
display mode, 85
  options, 85-87
:Display Colors Wysiwyg
  command, 82-83
:Display Default Wysiwyg
  command, 84
:Display Font-Directory Wysiwyg
  command, 84
:Display Mode Wysiwyg
  command, 85
:Display Options Wysiwyg
  command, 85-87

Index

:Display Rows Wysiwyg command, 87
:Display Zoom Wysiwyg command, 88
displaying
  colors, 82-83
  graphics, 103
  graphs, 46
  lists of files, 32
  print range as it will appear printed, 111
  rows, specifying number, 87
  worksheets, 78
    graphics, 103
    status, 79
    window, 80-81
  Wysiwyg print status screen, 108

E

Edit (F2) function key, 4
editing
  cell contents, 12
  graphs, 97-99
End+← key combination, 2
End+→ key combination, 2
End+↑ key combination, 2
End+↓ key combination, 2
End+Ctrl-Home key combination, 3
End+Ctrl-PgDn key combination, 3
End+Ctrl-PgUp key combination, 3
End+Home key combination, 2
enhancement add-ins, 123
erasing
  active files from memory, 71
  files from disks, 31
  range contents, 60
Esc 1-2-3 key, 6
exiting 1-2-3, 59
  temporarily, 69
exporting Wysiwyg format file, 114
external databases
  creating/deleting tables, 15
  linking to 1-2-3 databases, 18
  listing tables/fields in, 16
  sending commands directly to, 16-18

F

/File Admin Link-Refresh 1-2-3 command, 28
/File Admin Reservation 1-2-3 command, 29
/File Admin Seal 1-2-3 command, 29
/File Admin Table 1-2-3 command, 30
/File Combine 1-2-3 command, 30
/File Dir 1-2-3 command, 31
/File Erase 1-2-3 command, 31
/File Import 1-2-3 command, 31
/File List 1-2-3 command, 32
/File New 1-2-3 command, 33
/File Open 1-2-3 command, 33
/File Retrieve 1-2-3 command, 33
/File Save 1-2-3 command, 34-35
/File Xtract 1-2-3 command, 35
files
  blank, creating, 33
  combining values/formulas, 30
  controlling status on network, 29
  deleting, 70
  displaying lists, 32
  entering table of, 30
  erasing
    active files from memory, 71
    from disks, 31
  importing into worksheets, 31
  loading from disk, 33
  opening into memory, 33
  printing ranges to encoded files, 107
  protecting
    format, 29
    from change, 75
  saving, 34-35
  updating graphics in, 97
finding text, 67
font directory, specifying, 84
fonts, selecting, 90
footers, printing, 54
:Fomat Bold Wysiwyg command, 89
:Format Color Wysiwyg command, 89
:Format Font Wysiwyg command, 90
:Format Italics Wysiwyg command, 91

:Format Lines Wysiwyg command, 92-93
:Format Reset Wysiwyg command, 93
:Format Shade Wysiwyg command, 94
:Format Underline Wysiwyg command, 94
:Format Wysiwyg command, 8
formats
  applying to multiple worksheets, 74
  copying, 13
  default numeric, 74
  file, protecting, 29
  moving, 116
  Wysiwyg, copying, 114
formatting
  codes, sending to printers, 57
  ranges, 60-62
  Wysiwyg, removing, 93
formulas
  combining, 30
  copying, 13
  entering, 10-12
  generating tables from, 26-27
  identifying, 124
  recalculating, 28
  replacing with values, 69
  specifying value formulas should equal, 127
Formulas Auditor add-in, 124
Formulas-Cell Backsolver add-in, 126
function key combinations, 4-5
functions, 1-2-3, 133-137

G

GoTo (F5) function key, 3-4
Graph (F10) function key, 5
:Graph Add Wysiwyg command, 95
:Graph Compute Wysiwyg command, 97
:Graph Edit Wysiwyg command, 97-99
:Graph Goto Wysiwyg command, 99
/Graph Group 1-2-3 command, 37
:Graph Move Wysiwyg command, 99
/Graph Name 1-2-3 command, 37
/Graph Options Advanced Colors 1-2-3 command, 38
/Graph Options Advanced Hatches 1-2-3 command, 39
/Graph Options Advanced Text 1-2-3 command, 39
/Graph Options Color/B&W 1-2-3 command, 40
/Graph Options Data-Labels 1-2-3 command, 41
/Graph Options Format 1-2-3 command, 41
/Graph Options Grid 1-2-3 command, 42
/Graph Options Legend 1-2-3 command, 42
/Graph Options Scale 1-2-3 command, 43
/Graph Options Titles 1-2-3 command, 43
:Graph Remove Wysiwyg command, 100
/Graph Reset 1-2-3 command, 44
/Graph Save 1-2-3 command, 44
:Graph Settings Wysiwyg command, 101-103
/Graph Type 1-2-3 command, 44-46
/Graph View 1-2-3 command, 46
:Graph View Wysiwyg command, 103
/Graph X/A/B/C/D/E/F 1-2-3 command, 36
:Graph Zoom Wysiwyg command, 103
graphics
  adding to worksheets, 95
  deleting from worksheets, 100
  displaying, 103
  moving, 99
  moving cell pointer to, 99
  updating in active files, 97
  worksheet graphics, displaying, 103
graphs
  changing
    fonts/size/color of text, 39
    shading for ranges, 39
  colors
    for data ranges, 38
    used to display, 40
  data ranges, 37
  displaying, 46

Index

editing, 97-99
enhancing, 51-53
identifying/connecting data
    points, 41
labeling graph points, 41
legends, 42
overlaying grids, 42
saving, 44
scales, 43
selecting for printing, 50
settings
    cancelling, 44
    specifying, 101-103
    storing, 37
titles, 43
types, 44-46
grids, on graphs, 42

H

headers, printing, 54
Help (F1) function key, 4
highlighting ranges with mouse, 8
Home key, 2

I

icons, selecting with mouse, 6
importing
    ASCII files, 31
    from Wysiwyg format files,
        115-116
installing mouse, 6
inverting columns/rows, 19
italicizing data, 91

J-K

justifying text, 63

keys
    1-2-3, 5-6
    function, 4-5
    pointer, 1-4

L

labels
    aligning text, 64
        globally, 75
    changing alignment of, 117
    copying, 13
    entering, 9

in specified ranges, 118
justifying column of, 119
prefixes, 9
separating, 19
Link Viewer add-in, 132
loading
    add-in into memory, 81
    files from disks, 33

M

macro key names, 137-139
margins, setting for printing, 55
menu commands, selecting, 7
mouse, 6-8
/Move 1-2-3 command, 46
moving
    cell pointer
        to graphics, 99
        with mouse, 7
    data, 46
    formats, 116
    graphics, 99
multiple worksheets, pointer
    keys, 3

N

Name (F3) function key, 4
:Named-Style Wysiwyg
    command, 104
naming print settings, 55-57
Num Lock key, 1-2
numbers, entering, 10
numeric
    formats, defining default, 74
    operators, 11

O

Open Viewer add-in, 132
opening files into memory, 33
Options Auditor add-in, 124, 125
Options Solver add-in, 129
output range, copying to, 21

P

page breaks, 79, 121-122
page layout, 108-110
PgDn key, 2
PgUp key, 2
pointer keys, 1-4

Precedents Auditor add-in, 125
/Print 1-2-3 command, 47
:Print Configuration Wysiwyg command, 105-106
:Print File Wysiwyg command, 107
:Print Go Wysiwyg command, 107
:Print Info Wysiwyg command, 108
:Print Layout Wysiwyg command, 108-110
:Print Preview Wysiwyg command, 111
/Print Printer /File/Encoded 1-2-3 command, 47
/Print Printer Align 1-2-3 command, 48
/Print Printer Clear 1-2-3 command, 49
/Print Printer Hold 1-2-3 command, 49
/Print Printer Image 1-2-3 command, 50
/Print Printer Line 1-2-3 command, 50
/Print Printer Options Advance 1-2-3 command, 51-53
/Print Printer Options Borders 1-2-3 command, 54
/Print Printer Options Footer/Header 1-2-3 command, 54
/Print Printer Options Margins 1-2-3 command, 55
/Print Printer Options Name 1-2-3 command, 55-57
/Print Printer Options Other 1-2-3 command, 57
/Print Printer Options Pg-Length 1-2-3 command, 57
/Print Printer Options Setup 1-2-3 command, 57
/Print Printer Page 1-2-3 command, 58
/Print Printer Range 1-2-3 command, 58
/Print Printer Sample 1-2-3 command, 59
print range, specifying/cancelling, 111-112
:Print Range Wysiwyg command, 111-112

print settings
　clearing, 49
　naming, 55-57
　specifying, 112-113
:Print Settings Wysiwyg command, 112-113
printers
　advancing line by line, 50
　controlling paper feed, 58
　sending
　　data to, 107
　　formatting codes to, 57
　synchronizing with 1-2-3, 48
printing
　columns on every page, 54
　defining area to print, 58
　enhancing, 51-53
　footers, 54
　graphs, 50
　headers, 54
　putting jobs on hold, 49
　ranges
　　to encoded files, 107
　　to printers, 47
　rows on every page, 54
　sample pages, 59
　selecting format for cells, 57
　setting margins, 55
　specifying
　　number of lines per page, 57
　　print configuration options, 105-106
　taking jobs off hold, 49
prompt line, 1

Q

Query (F7) function key, 4
/Quit 1-2-3 command, 59
:Quit Wysiwyg command, 113

R

/Range Erase 1-2-3 command, 60
/Range Format 1-2-3 command, 60-62
/Range Input 1-2-3 command, 63
/Range Justify 1-2-3 command, 63
/Range Label 1-2-3 command, 64
/Range Name 1-2-3 command, 64-66
/Range Prot/Unprot 1-2-3 command, 66

/Range Search 1-2-3 command, 67
/Range Trans 1-2-3 command, 68
/Range Value 1-2-3 command, 69
ranges
  adding
  changing protection status, 66
  creating range names, 64-66
  entering/editing labels in, 118
  erasing contents, 60
  filling, 18
  formatting, 60-62
  highlighting with mouse, 8
  input, 23
  print, 111-112
  removing records from, 21
  searching, 23
  shading, 94
  specifying, 7-8
  text, 117
  underlining, 94
READY mode, returning 1-2-3 to, 113
Recalc-List Auditor add-in, 125
recalculation order, identifying, 125
Record (Alt-F2) function key, 5
records
  copying, 24
  inserting/replacing in input range from output range, 23
  removing from ranges, 21
  searching for in databases, 22
  specifying records to be searched, 23
replacing text, 67
Report Solver add-in, 130-131
reservation status, 29
Retrieve Viewer add-in, 133
rows
  deleting, 70
  inserting, 78
  inverting, 19
  printing on every page, 54
  specifying
    height, 122
    number to be displayed, 87
Run (Alt-F3) function key, 5

S

saving
  files, 34-35
  graphs, 44

Scroll Lock key, 3
Solve Backsolver add-in, 127
Solve Solver add-in, 131
Solver add-in, 127
sorting data, 25
:Special Copy Wysiwyg command, 114
:Special Export Wysiwyg command, 114
:Special Import Wysiwyg command, 115-116
:Special Move Wysiwyg command, 116
string operators, 12
styles, defining/applying, 104
/System 1-2-3 command, 69

T

Tab key, 2
Table (F8) function key, 4
tables, creating, 26-27
  labeled, 27-28
  of files, 30
text
  color, 89
  finding and replacing, 67
  justifying, 63
  labels, aligning, 64
  range, 119
:Text Align Wysiwyg command, 117
:Text Clear Wysiwyg command, 117
:Text Edit Wysiwyg command, 118
:Text Reformat Wysiwyg command, 119
:Text Set Wysiwyg command, 119
:Text Wysiwyg command, 8
titles, freezing on-screen, 79
transposing data, 68

U-V

Undo (Alt-F4) function key, 5

Value Backsolver add-in, 127
values
  combining, 30
  replacing formulas, 69
Viewer add-in, 132

W

Window (F6) function key, 3-4
/Worksheet Column 1-2-3 command, 70
:Worksheet Column Wysiwyg command, 120-121
/Worksheet Delete 1-2-3 command, 70
/Worksheet Erase 1-2-3 command, 71
/Worksheet Global Default 1-2-3 command, 71-73
/Worksheet Global Format 1-2-3 command, 74
/Worksheet Global Group 1-2-3 command, 74
/Worksheet Global Label 1-2-3 command, 75
/Worksheet Global Prot 1-2-3 command, 75
/Worksheet Global Recalc 1-2-3 command, 76-77
/Worksheet Global Zero 1-2-3 command, 77
/Worksheet Global-Col Width 1-2-3 command, 71
/Worksheet Hide 1-2-3 command, 78
/Worksheet Insert 1-2-3 command, 78
/Worksheet Page 1-2-3 command, 79
:Worksheet Page Wysiwyg command, 121-122
:Worksheet Row Wysiwyg command, 122
/Worksheet Status 1-2-3 command, 79
/Worksheet Titles 1-2-3 command, 79
/Worksheet Window 1-2-3 command, 80-81
worksheets
  adding
    graphics, 95
    lines to, 92-93
  analyzing, 123
  applying one format to all worksheets in file, 74
  defining recalculation, 76-77
  deleting, 70
    graphics from, 100
  displaying, 78
    status, 79
    worksheet window, 80-81
  enlarging/reducing cells, 88
  freezing titles on-screen, 79
  hiding, 78
  importing files, 31
  inserting, 78
    page breaks manually, 79
  multiple, 3
  pointer keys, 2-3
  protecting from change, 75
  setting global column width, 71
  specifying
    default settings, 71-73
    ranges, 20, 36
  supressing display of zeros, 77
Wysiwyg
  format
    copying, 114
    removing, 93
  print status screen, 108

X-Z

Zoom (Alt-F6) function key, 5